The Cobra's Heart

The heat of the Serengeti Plain, 1962

RYSZARD KAPUŚCIŃSKI

The Cobra's Heart

Translated by KLARA GLOWCZEWSKA

GREAT
JOURNEYS

TED SMART

PENGUIN BOOKS

Published by the Penguin Group
Penguin Books Ltd, 80 Strand, London WC2R ORL, England
Penguin Group (USA) Inc., 375 Hudson Street, New York, New York 10014, USA
Penguin Group (Canada), 90 Eglinton Avenue East, Suite 700, Toronto, Ontario, Canada M4P 2Y3
(a division of Pearson Penguin Canada Inc.)
Penguin Ireland, 25 St Stephen's Green, Dublin 2, Ireland (a division of Penguin Books Ltd)
Penguin Group (Australia), 250 Camberwell Road, Camberwell, Victoria 3124, Australia
(a division of Pearson Australia Group Pty Ltd)
Penguin Books India Pvt Ltd, 11 Community Centre, Panchsheel Park, New Delhi – 110 017, India
Penguin Group (NZ), 67 Apollo Drive, Rosedale, North Shore 0632, New Zealand
(a division of Pearson New Zealand Ltd)
Penguin Books (South Africa) (Pty) Ltd, 24 Sturdee Avenue, Rosebank, Johannesburg 2196, South Africa

Penguin Books Ltd, Registered Offices: 80 Strand, London WC2R ORL, England

www.penguin.com

Heben first published in Poland 1998
First published in the USA under the title *The Shadow of the Sun* by
Alfred A. Knopf 2001
First published in Great Britain by Allen Lane 2001
This extract first published in Penguin Books 2007

3

Copyright © Ryszard Kapuściński, 1998
Translation copyright © Klara Glowczewska, 2001
All rights reserved

The moral rights of the author and translator have been asserted

This book published in Canada with
the kind permission of Random House, Inc.

Taken from the Penguin Modern Classics edition of *The Shadow of the Sun*,
translated by Klara Glowczewska

Typeset by Rowland Phototypesetting Ltd, Bury St Edmunds, Suffolk
Printed in England by Clays Ltd, St Ives plc

ISBN: 978-0-141-02555-1

This edition produced for The Book People Ltd,
Hall Wood Avenue, Haydock, St. Helens, WA11 9UL

Contents

I lived in Africa for several years. I first went there in 1957. Then, over the next forty years, I returned whenever the opportunity arose. I travelled extensively, avoiding official routes, palaces, important personages, and high-level politics. Instead, I opted to hitch rides on passing trucks, wander with nomads through the desert, be the guest of peasants of the tropical savannah. Their life is endless toil, a torment they endure with astonishing patience and good humour.

This is therefore not a book about Africa, but rather about some people from there – about encounters with them, and time spent together. The continent is too large to describe. It is a veritable ocean, a separate planet, a varied, immensely rich cosmos. Only with the greatest simplification, for the sake of convenience, can we say 'Africa'. In reality, except as a geographical appellation, Africa does not exist.

R. K.

The Beginning:
Collision, Ghana, 1958

More than anything, one is struck by the light. Light everywhere. Brightness everywhere. Everywhere, the sun. Just yesterday, an autumnal London was drenched in rain. The aeroplane drenched in rain. A cold wind, darkness. But here, from the morning's earliest moments, the airport is ablaze with sunlight, all of us in sunlight.

In times past, when people wandered the world on foot, rode on horseback, or sailed in ships, the journey itself accustomed them to the change. Images of the earth passed ever so slowly before their eyes, the stage revolved in a barely perceptible way. The voyage lasted weeks, months. The traveller had time to grow used to another environment, a different landscape. The climate, too, changed gradually. Before the traveller arrived from a cool Europe at the burning Equator, he already had left behind the pleasant warmth of Las Palmas, the heat of Al-Mahara, and the hell of the Cape Verde Islands.

Today, nothing remains of these gradations. Air travel tears us violently out of snow and cold and hurls us that very same day into the blaze of the tropics. Suddenly, still rubbing our eyes, we find ourselves in a humid inferno. We immediately start to sweat. If we've come from Europe in the wintertime, we discard overcoats, peel off sweaters. It's the first gesture of initiation we, the people of the North, perform upon arrival in Africa.

People of the North. Have we sufficiently considered the fact that northerners constitute a distinct minority on our planet? Canadians and Poles, Lithuanians and Scandinavians, some Americans and Germans, Russians and Scots, Laplanders and Eskimos, Evenkis and Yakuts – the list is not very long. It may amount to no more than 500 million people: less than 10 percent of the earth's population. The overwhelming majority live in hot climates, their days spent in the warmth of the sun. Mankind first came into being in the sun; the oldest traces of his existence have been found in warm climes. What was the weather like in the biblical paradise? It was eternally warm, hot even, so that Adam and Eve could go about naked and not feel chilled even in the shade of a tree.

Something else strikes the new arrival even as he descends the steps of the aeroplane: the smell of the tropics. Perhaps he's had intimations of it. It is the scent that permeated Mr Kanzman's little shop, Colonial and Other Goods, on Perec Street in my hometown of Pińsk. Almonds, cloves, dates, and cocoa. Vanilla and laurel leaves, oranges and bananas, cardamom and saffron. And Drohobych. The interiors of Bruno Schulz's cinnamon shops? Didn't their 'dimly lit, dark, and solemn interiors' smell intensely of paints, lacquer, incense, the aroma of faraway countries and rare substances? Yet the actual smell of the tropics is somewhat different. We instantly recognize its weight, its sticky materiality. The smell makes us at once aware that we are at that point on earth where an exuberant and indefatigable nature labours, incessantly reproducing itself, spreading and blooming, even as it sickens, disintegrates, festers, and decays.

It is the smell of a sweating body and drying fish, of spoiling meat and roasting cassava, of fresh flowers and putrid algae – in short, of everything that is at once pleasant and irritating, that attracts and repels, seduces and disgusts. This odour will reach us from nearby palm groves, will escape from the hot soil, will waft above stagnant city sewers. It will not leave us; it is integral to the tropics.

And finally, the most important discovery – the people. The locals. How they fit this landscape, this light, these smells. How they are as one with them. How man and environment are bound in an indissoluble, complementary, and harmonious whole. I am struck by how firmly each race is grounded in the terrain in which it lives, in its climate. We shape our landscape, and it, in turn, moulds our physiognomy. Among these palm trees and vines, in this bush and jungle, the white man is a sort of outlandish and unseemly intruder. Pale, weak, his shirt drenched with sweat, his hair pasted down on his head, he is continually tormented by thirst, and feels impotent, melancholic. He is ever afraid: of mosquitoes, amoebas, scorpions, snakes – everything that moves fills him with fear, terror, panic.

With their strength, grace, and endurance, the in-

digenous move about naturally, freely, at a tempo
determined by climate and tradition, somewhat lan-
guid, unhurried, knowing one can never achieve everything in life anyway, and besides, if one did, what
would be left over for others?

I've been here for a week. I am trying to get to know
Accra. It is like an overgrown small town that has
reproduced itself many times over, crawled out of the
bush, out of the jungle, and come to a halt at the shores
of the Gulf of Guinea. Accra is flat, single-storeyed,
humble, though there are some buildings with two or
more floors. No sophisticated architecture, no excess
or pomp. Ordinary plaster, pastel-coloured walls – pale
yellow, pale green. The walls have numerous water
stains. Fresh ones. After the rainy season, entire con-
stellations of stains appear, collages, mosaics, fantastical maps, flowery flourishes. The downtown is densely
built up. Traffic, crowds, bustle – life takes place out
in the street. The street is a roadway delineated on
both sides by an open sewer. There are no sidewalks.
Cars mingle with the crowds. Everything moves in
concert – pedestrians, automobiles, bicycles, carts,
cows, and goats. On the sides, beyond the sewer, along
the entire length of the street, domestic scenes unfold.
Women are pounding manioc, baking taro bulbs over
the coals, cooking dishes of one sort or another, hawking chewing gum, crackers, and aspirin, washing and
drying laundry. Right out in the open, as if a decree
had been issued commanding everyone to leave his
home at 8 a.m. and remain in the street. In reality,

there is another reason: apartments are small, cramped, stuffy. There is no ventilation, the atmosphere inside is heavy, the smells stale, there is no air to breathe. Besides, spending the day in the street enables one to participate in social life. The women talk nonstop, yell, gesticulate, laugh. Standing over a pot or a washbasin, they have an excellent vantage point. They can see their neighbours, passersby, the entire street; they can listen in on quarrels and gossip, observe accidents. All day long they are among others, in motion, and in the fresh air.

A red Ford with a speaker mounted on its roof passes through the streets. A hoarse, penetrating voice invites people to attend a meeting. The main attraction will be Kwame Nkrumah-Osagyefo, the prime minister, the leader of Ghana, of Africa, of all downtrodden peoples. There are photographs of Nkrumah everywhere – in the newspapers (every day), on posters, on flags, on ankle-length percale skirts. The energetic face of a middle-aged man, either smiling or serious, at an angle meant to suggest that he is contemplating the future.

'Nkrumah is a saviour!' a young teacher named Joe Yambo tells me with rapture in his voice. 'Have you heard him speak? He sounds like a prophet!'

Yes, in fact, I had heard him. He arrived at the stadium with an entourage of his ministers – young, animated, they created the impression of people who were having a good time, who were full of joy. The ceremony began with priests pouring bottles of gin over the podium – it was an offering to the gods, a way of making contact with them, a plea for their favour, their goodwill. Among the adults in the audience there were also children, from infants strapped to their mothers' backs, to babies beginning to crawl, to toddlers and school-age children. The older ones take care of the younger ones, and those older ones are taken care of by ones older still. This hierarchy of age is strictly observed, and obedience is absolute. A four-year-old has full authority over a two-year-old, a six-year-old over a four-year-old. Children take care of children, so that the adults can devote themselves to their affairs – for instance, to listening carefully to Nkrumah.

Osagyefo spoke briefly. He said that the most important thing was to gain independence – everything else would follow naturally, all that is good would emerge from the very fact of independence.

A portly fellow, given to decisive gestures, he had shapely, expressive features and large, lively eyes, which moved over the sea of dark heads with an attention so concentrated as to suggest he wanted to count each and every one of them.

After the rally, those on the podium mingled with the audience. It was loud, chaotic, and there was no visible police protection or escort. Joe, who had brought me, elbowed his way towards a young man (whom he identified as a minister) and asked him if I could come to see him tomorrow. The other one, not really able to hear over the buzz and commotion what the issue was, replied, at least partially to get rid of us, 'Fine! Fine!'

6

The next day, I found my way to the Ministry of Education and Information, a new building set amid a growth of royal palms. It was Friday. On Saturday, sitting in my small hotel, I wrote a description of the preceding day:

The way is open: neither policeman, nor secretary, nor doors.

I draw aside a patterned curtain and enter. The minister's office is warm. In semidarkness, he is standing at his desk organizing his papers: crumpling those he will throw into the wastepaper basket, smoothing out others to place in his briefcase. A thin, slight figure, in a sports shirt, short trousers, sandals, with a flowery kente cloth draped over his left shoulder; nervous gestures.

This is Kofi Baako, minister of education and information.

At thirty-two, he is the youngest minister in Ghana, in the entire British Commonwealth, and he has already had his portfolio for three years now. His office is on the third floor of the ministry building. The hierarchy of positions is reflected in the ladder of floors. The higher the personage, the higher the floor. Fittingly, since on top there is a breeze, while towards the bottom the air is heavy as stone, motionless. Petty bureaucrats suffocate on the ground floor; above them, the departmental directors enjoy a slight draft; and at the very top, the delicious breeze caresses the ministers.

Anyone who wants to can come and see a minister whenever he wants to. If someone has a problem, he

travels to Accra, finds out where, for instance, the
minister of agriculture can be found. He goes to his
office, parts the curtain, sits down, and sets forth in
detail what's bothering him. If he doesn't find the
official at the agency, he will find him at home – even
better, because there he'll get a meal and something to
drink. People felt a remoteness from the white administration. But now these are their own people, they
don't have to feel inhibited. It's my government, so it
must help me. If it's to help me, it has to know the
situation. For it to know, I have to come and explain.
It's best that I do this on my own, in person and direct.

There is no end of these supplicants.

'Good morning!' said Kofi Baako. 'And where are
you from?'

'From Warsaw.'

'You know, I almost went there. I was travelling all
over Europe: France, Belgium, England, Yugoslavia. I
was in Czechoslovakia, about to go to Poland, when
Kwame sent me a telegram calling me back for the
party congress, our ruling Convention People's Party.'

We were sitting at a table, in his doorless office.
Instead of window panes there were shutters with
widely spaced slats, through which a gentle breeze
passed. The small room was piled high with papers,
files, brochures. A large safe stood in a corner, several
portraits of Nkrumah hung on the walls, a speaker
wired to a central system stood on a shelf. Tomtoms
pounded from it, until finally Baako turned it off.

I wanted him to tell me about himself, about his
life. Baako enjoys great prestige among the young.

They like him for being a good athlete. He plays soccer, cricket, and is Ghana's ping-pong champion.

'Just a minute,' he interrupted, 'I just have to place a call to Kumasi, because I'm going there tomorrow for a game.'

He called the post office for them to connect him. They told him to wait.

'I saw two films yesterday,' he told me, as he waited, holding the receiver to his ear. 'I wanted to see what they're showing. They're playing films schoolchildren shouldn't go to. I must issue a decree that forbids young people to see such things. And this morning I spent visiting book stalls throughout the city. The government has established low prices for schoolbooks, but the word is that retailers are marking them up. I went to check for myself. Indeed, they are selling them for more than they're supposed to.'

He dialled the post office again.

'Listen, what are you so busy with over there? How long am I supposed to wait? Do you know who this is?'

A woman's voice answered, 'No.'

'And who are you?' Baako asked.

'I'm the telephone operator.'

'And I am the minister of education and information, Kofi Baako.'

'Good morning, Kofi! I'll connect you right away.'

And he was talking to Kumasi.

I looked at his books, stacked on a small cabinet: Hemingway, Lincoln, Koestler, Orwell, *The Popular History of Music*, *The American Dictionary*, as well as various paperbacks and crime novels.

'Reading is my passion. In England I bought myself the *Encyclopaedia Britannica*, and now I'm reading it little by little. I cannot eat without reading, I have to have a book lying open in front of me.'

A moment later:

'I've got another, even greater hobby: photography. I take pictures all the time and everywhere. I have more than ten cameras. When I go to a store and see a new camera, I immediately have to buy it. I bought a film projector for the children, and show them films in the evening.'

He has four children, ranging in age from three to nine. All of them attend school, even the youngest. It is not unusual here for a three-year-old to be enrolled in school. The mother will send him off, especially if he's a handful, just to have some peace.

Kofi Baako himself first went to school at three. His father was a teacher and liked being able to keep his eye on his children. When he finished elementary school, he was sent for high school to Cape Coast. He became a teacher, and then a civil servant. At the end of 1947, Nkrumah had returned to Ghana having finished university studies in America and England. Baako listened to his speeches, which spoke of independence. Then Baako wrote an article, 'My Hatred of Imperialism'. He was fired from his job. He was blacklisted, and no one would employ him. He hung around the city, eventually meeting Nkrumah, who entrusted him with the position of editor-in-chief of the *Cape Coast Daily Mail*. Kofi was twenty years old.

He wrote another article entitled 'We Call for Freedom', and was jailed. Arrested with him were Nkrumah and several other activists. They spent thirteen months behind bars, before finally being released. Today, this group constitutes Ghana's government.

Now Baako speaks about broad issues. 'Only thirty percent of the people in Ghana can read and write. We want to abolish illiteracy within fifteen years. There are difficulties: a shortage of teachers, books, schools. There are two kinds of schools: missionary-run and state-run. But they are all subject to the state and there is a single educational policy. In addition, five thousand students are being educated abroad. What frequently happens is that they return and no longer share a common language with the people. Look at the opposition. Its leaders are Oxford- and Cambridge-educated.'

'What does the opposition want?'

'Who knows? We believe that an opposition is necessary. The leader of the opposition in parliament receives a salary from the government. We allowed all these little opposition parties and groups to unite, so they would be stronger. Our position is that in Ghana, anyone who wants to has the right to form a political party – on the condition that it not be based on criteria of race, religion, or tribe. Each party here can employ all constitutional means to gain political power. But, you understand, despite all this, one doesn't know what the opposition wants. They call a meeting and shout: "We've come through Oxford, and people like Kofi Baako didn't even finish high school. Today Baako is a minister, and I am nothing. But when I become minister, then Baako will be too stupid for me to make him even a messenger." But you know, people don't listen to this kind of talk, because there are more Kofi Baakos here than all those in the opposition put together.'

I said that I should get going, as it was dinnertime. He asked me what I was doing that evening. I was supposed to go to Togo.

'What for?' He waved his hand. 'Come to a party. The radio station is having one tonight.'

I didn't have an invitation. He looked around for a piece of paper and wrote: 'Admit Ryszard Kapuściński, a journalist from Poland, to your party. Kofi Baako, Minister of Education and Information.'

'There. I'll be there too, we'll take some photographs.'

The guard at the gates of the radio building saluted me smartly and I was promptly seated at a special table. The party was already in full swing when a grey Peugeot drove up to the dance floor out in the garden, and Kofi Baako emerged from inside. He was dressed just as he had been in his office, only he held a red sweat suit under his arm, because he was going to Kumasi tonight and it might get cold. He was well known here. Baako was the minister of schools, of all the universities, the press, the radio, the publishing houses, the museums – of everything that constitutes culture, art, and propaganda in this country.

We soon found ourselves in a crowd. He sat down to drink a Coca-Cola, then quickly stood up.

'Come, I will show you my cameras.'

He pulled a suitcase out of the boot of his car, set it on the ground, knelt down, and began taking out the cameras, laying them out on the grass. There were fifteen of them.

Just then two boys walked up to us, slightly drunk.

'Kofi,' one of them began in a plaintive tone, 'we bought a ticket and they're not letting us stay here because we don't have jackets. So what did they sell us a ticket for?'

Baako rose.

'Listen,' he answered, 'I am too important a man for such matters. There are lots of little guys here, let them take care of it. I have issues of government on my mind.'

The twosome sailed off unsteadily, and we went to take pictures. Baako had only to approach, cameras hanging around his neck, for people to start calling to him, asking for a photograph.

'Kofi, take one of us.'

'Of us!'

'And us too!'

He circulated, picking tables with the prettiest girls, arranging them, and telling them to smile. He knew them by name: Abena, Ekua, Esi. They greeted him by extending their hands, without getting up, and shrugging their shoulders, which is an expression of seductive flirtatiousness here. Baako walked on; we took many photographs. He looked at his watch.

'I have to go.'

He wanted to get to the game on time.

'Come tomorrow, and we'll develop the photographs.'
The Peugeot flashed its lights and vanished in the darkness, while the party swayed and surged till dawn.

The Road to Kumasi

What does the bus station in Accra most resemble? The caravan of a huge circus that has come to a brief stop. It is colourful, and there is music. The buses are more like circus wagons than the luxurious vehicles that roll along the highways of Europe and North America.

A bus in Accra has a wooden body, its roof resting on four posts. Because there are open walls, a pleasant breeze cools the ride. In this climate, the value of a breeze is never to be taken for granted.

In the Sahara, the palaces of rulers have the most ingenious constructions – full of chinks, crannies, winding passageways, and corridors so conceived and constructed as to maximize cross-ventilation. In the afternoon heat, the ruler reclines on a mat optimally positioned to catch this refreshing current, which he breathes with delight. A breeze is a financially measurable commodity: the most expensive houses are built where the breeze is best. Still air has no value; it has only to move, however, and then it immediately acquires a price.

The buses are brightly ornamented, colourfully painted. On the cabs and along the sides, crocodiles bare their sharp teeth, snakes stretch ready to attack, and flocks of peacocks frolic in trees, while antelope race through the savannah pursued by a lion. Birds are everywhere, as well as garlands, bouquets of flowers. It's kitsch, but full of imagination and life.

The inscriptions are most important of all. The words, adorned with flowers, are large and legible from afar, meant to offer important encouragements or warnings. They have to do with God, mankind, guilt, taboos.

The spiritual world of the 'African' (if one may use the term despite its gross simplification) is rich and complex, and his inner life is permeated by a profound religiosity. He believes in the coexistence of three different yet related worlds.

The first is the one that surrounds us, the palpable and visible reality composed of living people, animals, and plants, as well as inanimate objects: stones, water, air. The second is the world of the ancestors, those who died before us, but who died, as it were, not completely, not finally, not absolutely. Indeed, in a metaphysical sense they continue to exist, and are even capable of participating in our life, of influencing it, shaping it. That is why maintaining good relations with one's ancestors is a precondition of a successful life, and sometimes even of life itself. The third world is the rich kingdom of the spirits – spirits that exist independently, yet at the same time are present in every being, in every object, in everything and everywhere.

At the head of these three worlds stands the Supreme Being, God. Many of the bus inscriptions speak of omnipresence and his unknown omnipotence:

'God is everywhere', 'God knows what he does', 'God is mystery'. There are also some more down-to-earth, human injunctions: 'Smile', 'Tell me that I'm beautiful', 'Those who bicker like each other', etc.

We have only to show up in the square, which teems with dozens of buses, before a group of shouting children surrounds us – where are we going? to Kumasi? to Takoradi? or to Tamale?

'To Kumasi.'

Those who are hunting for passengers to Kumasi shake our hands and, bouncing with glee, lead us to the appropriate bus. They are happy, because, having found him a passenger, the bus driver will reward them with a banana or an orange.

We climb into the bus and sit down. At this point there is a risk of culture clash, of collision and conflict. It will undoubtedly occur if the passenger is a foreigner who doesn't know Africa. Someone like that will start looking around, squirming, inquiring, 'When will the bus leave?'

'What do you mean, when?' the astonished driver will reply. 'It will leave when we find enough people to fill it up.'

The European and the African have an entirely different concept of time. In the European worldview, time exists outside man, exists objectively, and has measurable and linear characteristics. According to Newton, time is absolute: 'Absolute, true, mathematical time of itself and from its own nature, it flows equably and without relation to anything external.' The European feels himself to be time's slave, dependent on it, subject to it. To exist and function, he must observe its iron-clad, inviolate laws, its inflexible principles and rules. He must heed deadlines, dates, days, and hours. He moves within the rigours of time and cannot exist outside them. They impose upon him their require-ments and quotas. An unresolvable conflict exists between man and time, one that always ends with man's defeat – time annihilates him.

Africans apprehend time differently. For them, it is a much looser concept, more open, elastic, subjective. It is man who influences time, its shape, course, and rhythm (man acting, of course, with the consent of gods and ancestors). Time is even something that man can create outright, for time is made manifest through events, and whether an event takes place or not depends, after all, on man alone. If two armies do not engage in a battle, then that battle will not occur (in other words, time will not have revealed its presence, will not have come into being).

Time appears as a result of our actions, and vanishes when we neglect or ignore it. It is something that springs to life under our influence, but falls into a state of hibernation, even nonexistence, if we do not direct our energy toward it. It is a subservient, passive essence, and, most importantly, one dependent on man.

The absolute opposite of time as it is understood in the European worldview.

In practical terms, this means that if you go to a village where a meeting is scheduled for the afternoon but find no one at the appointed spot, asking, 'When will the meeting take place?' makes no sense. You know the answer: 'It will take place when people come.'

Therefore the African who boards a bus sits down in a vacant seat, and immediately falls into a state in which he spends a great portion of his life: a benumbed waiting.

'These people have a fantastic talent for waiting!' an Englishman who has lived here for years tells me. 'Talent, stamina, some peculiar kind of instinct.'

Africans believe that a mysterious energy circulates through the world, ebbing and flowing, and if it draws near and fills us up, it will give us the strength to set time into motion – something will start to happen. Until this occurs, however, one must wait; any other behaviour is delusional and quixotic.

What does this dull waiting consist of? People know what to expect; therefore, they try to settle themselves in as comfortably as possible, in the best possible place. Sometimes they lie down, sometimes they sit on the ground, or on a stone, or squat. They stop talking. A waiting group is mute. It emits no sound. The body goes limp, droops, shrinks. The muscles relax. The neck stiffens, the head ceases to move. The person does not look around, does not observe anything, is not curious. Sometimes his eyes are closed – but not always. More frequently, they are open but appear unseeing, with no spark of life in them. I have observed for hours on end crowds of people in this state of inanimate waiting, a kind of profound physiological sleep: they do not eat, they do not drink, they do not urinate; they react neither to the mercilessly scorching sun, nor to the aggressive, voracious flies that cover their eyelids and lips.

What, in the meantime, is going on inside their heads?

I do not know. Are they thinking? Dreaming? Reminiscing? Making plans? Meditating? Travelling in the world beyond? It is difficult to say.

Finally, after two hours of waiting, the bus, now packed full, leaves the station. On the rough potholed road, shaken this way and that, the passengers come to life. Someone reaches for a biscuit, someone else peels a banana. People look around, wipe sweaty faces, neatly fold wet handkerchiefs. The driver is talking nonstop, holding the steering wheel with one hand, gesticulating with the other. Everyone keeps bursting out in laughter, the driver the loudest, the others more softly; perhaps they're just doing it out of politeness, because they feel they should.

We're on our way. My fellow passengers are only the second, perhaps even the first generation of Africans fortunate enough to be conveyed to their destinations. For thousands and thousands of years, Africa walked. People here did not have a concept of the wheel, and were unable to adopt it. They walked, they wandered, and whatever had to be transported they carried – on their backs, on their shoulders, and, most often, on their heads.

How is it that during the nineteenth century there

were ships on lakes deep in the interior of the continent? They were first disassembled at oceanic ports, then carried piecemeal on people's heads and put back together again on the shores of the lakes. Cities, factories, mining equipment, electrical plants, hospitals, all were carried in sections deep into Africa. All the products of nineteenth-century technology were transported into Africa's interior on the heads of its inhabitants.

The people of northern Africa, even of the Sahara, were more fortunate in this respect: they could use a beast of burden, the camel. But neither the camel nor the horse was able to adapt to regions south of the Sahara – they perished, decimated by the encephalitis borne by the tsetse fly, as well as by other fatal diseases of the tropics.

The problem of Africa is the dissonance between the environment and the human being, between the immensity of African space (more than thirty million square kilometres!) and the defenceless, barefoot, wretched man who inhabits it. Whichever direction he turns, there is distance, emptiness, wilderness, boundlessness. Often one had to walk for hundreds, thousands of miles to encounter other people (to say 'another human being' would be inappropriate, for a lone individual could not survive in these conditions). For the most part information, knowledge, technological innovation, goods, commodities, and the experiences of others did not penetrate here, could not find a way in. Exchange as a means of participating in world culture did not exist. If it appeared, it did so only accidentally, as a rare event, an exception. And without exchange there is no progress.

Most frequently, people lived in small groups, clans, tribes isolated and scattered over vast, hostile territories, in mortal peril from malaria, drought, heat, hunger.

Living and moving about in small groups allowed them to flee danger more easily and thereby survive. These peoples applied the same tactic once practised by light cavalry on the European field of battle: the keys were mobility, the avoidance of head-on confrontation, the skirting and outsmarting of peril. As a consequence, the African was a man on the move. Even if he led a sedentary life in a village, he was also on the move, for periodically the entire village would set off: either the water had run out, or the soil had ceased to bear crops, or an epidemic had broken out, and off they would go, in search of succour, in the hope of finding something better. Only city life brought them a measure of stability.

The population of Africa was a gigantic, matted, criss-crossing web, spanning the entire continent and in constant motion, endlessly undulating, bunching up in one place and spreading out in another, a rich fabric, a colourful arras.

This compulsory mobility of the population resulted in Africa's interior having no old cities, at least none comparable in age to those that still exist in Europe, the Middle East, or Asia. Similarly – again in contrast to those other regions – many African societies (some claim all of them) today occupy terrain that they did not previously inhabit.

All are arrivals from elsewhere, all are immigrants. Africa is their common world, but within its boundaries they wandered and shifted about for centuries, a process that continues in certain parts of the continent to this day. Hence the striking physical characteristic of civilization is its temporariness, its provisional character, its material discontinuity. A hut put up only yesterday has already vanished. A field still cultivated three months ago is today lying fallow.

The continuity that lives and breathes here, and that creates the threads of the social fabric, is the continuity of family tradition and ritual, and the pervasive and far-reaching cult of the ancestor. Rather than a material or territorial community, it is a spiritual community that binds the African to those closest to him.

The bus is going deeper and deeper into the thick, tall, tropical forest. Biology in the temperate zones exhibits discipline and order: there is a little stand of pines here, some oaks over there, and birch trees somewhere else. Even in mixed forests a certain clarity and propriety prevail. In the tropics, however, the flora exists in a state of frenzy, in an ecstasy of the most untrammelled procreation. One is struck immediately by a cocky, pushy abundance, an endless eruption of an exuberant, panting mass of vegetation, all the elements of which – tree, bush, liana, vine, growing, pressing, stimulating, inciting one another – have already become so interlocked, knotted, and clenched that only sharpened steel, wielded with a horrendous amount of physical force, can cut through it a passage, path, or tunnel.

Because in the past there was no wheeled transport on this enormous continent, there were also no roads. When the first cars were brought here, early in the twentieth century, they didn't really have anywhere to go. A paved road is something new in Africa, at most several decades old. And in certain areas it still remains a rarity. Instead of roads, there were trails, usually shared by people and cattle alike. This age-old system of paths explains why people here are still in the habit of walking single file, even if they're travelling along one of today's wide roads. It explains, too, why a walking group is silent – it is difficult to conduct a conversation single file.

One can't afford to be less than a great expert on the geography of these paths. Whoever knows them less than well will lose his way, and if forced to wander too long without water and food will of course perish. Various clans, tribes, and villages have their own paths, which cross one another, and someone unfamiliar with their points of intersection can walk along one assuming it is taking him in the right direction, while in fact it may be leading him astray, even towards death. The most perplexing and dangerous are jungle paths. You are constantly caught on thorns and branches, reaching a destination all scratched and swollen. It is a good idea to carry a stick, for if a snake is lying across the path (as happens often), you must scare it off, and this is best accomplished with a stick. Talismans present further dilemmas. Inhabitants of the tropical forest, living in an impenetrable wilderness, are by nature wary and superstitious. To scare off evil spirits, they hang all kinds of talismans along the pathways. What should you do when you come upon a lizard's skin left hanging, a bird's head, a bunch of grass, or a crocodile's tooth? Should you risk continuing, or, rather, turn back, knowing that beyond this warning sign something truly evil might be lurking?

Every now and then our bus stops along the side of the road. Someone wants to get off. If it's a young woman with a child or two (a young woman without a child is a rare sight), there unfolds a scene of extraordinary agility and grace. First, the woman will secure the child to her body with a calico scarf (her small charge sleeping the entire time, not reacting). Next, she will squat down and place the bowl from which she is never separated, full of food and goods of all kinds, on her head. Then, straightening up, she will execute that manoeuvre of a tightrope walker taking his first step above the abyss: carefully, she finds her equilibrium. With her left hand she now clutches a woven sleeping mat, and with her right the hand of a second child. And this way – stepping at once with a very smooth, even gait – they enter a forest path leading to a world I do not know and perhaps will never understand.

*

My neighbour on the bus. A young man. An accountant from a firm in Kumasi whose name I don't catch.

'Ghana is independent!' he says ecstatically. 'Tomorrow, Africa will be independent!' he assures me. 'We are free!'

And he shakes my hand in a way meant to signify that now a black man can offer a white man his hand without self-consciousness.

'Did you see Nkrumah?' he asks, interested. 'Yes? Then you are a lucky man! Do you know what we'll do with the enemies of Africa?'

He laughs, ha-ha, but doesn't say exactly what will be done.

'Now the most important thing is education. Education, schooling, the acquiring of knowledge. We are so backward, so backward! I think that the whole world will come to our aid. We must be the equals of the developed countries. Not only free – but also equal. But for now, we are breathing freedom. And this is paradise. This is wonderful!'

This enthusiasm of his is universal here. Enthusiasm, and pride that Ghana stands at the head of the independence movement, sets an example, leads all of Africa.

My other neighbour, sitting to my left (the bus has three seats in a row), is different: withdrawn, taciturn, unengaged. He immediately draws attention to himself, for people here are generally open, eager to converse, quick to tell stories and deliver various opinions. Thus far he has told me only that he is working and that he is having some troubles at work. What sorts of troubles, he's not saying.

Finally, however, as the great forest starts to shrink and grow thinner, signalling that we are slowly approaching Kumasi, he decides to confess something to me. So – he has problems. He is sick. He is not sick always, not continously, but intermittently, periodically. He has already been to see various native specialists, but none of them has been able to help him. The thing is that he has animals in his head, under his skull. It's not that he sees these animals, that he thinks about them or is afraid of them. No. It's nothing like that. The animals are literally in his head; they live there, run around, graze, hunt, or just sleep. If they happen to be gentle animals, like antelopes, zebras, or giraffes, he tolerates them well; it is even quite pleasant then. But sometimes a hungry lion arrives. He is hungry, he is furious – so he roars. And then this roar makes his head explode.

I, a White Man

In Dar es Salaam I bought an old Land Rover from an Englishman who was returning to Europe. It was 1962, several months after Tanganyika had gained independence, and many Englishmen from the colonial administration had lost their jobs, positions, even houses. In their increasingly deserted clubs, someone was always recounting how he had walked into his office at the ministry, and there, smiling at him from behind his desk, was one of the locals. 'Excuse me. I'm very sorry!'

This changing of the guard is called Africanization. There are those who applaud it as a symbol of liberation, while others are outraged by the process. It is clear who is for and who is against. London and Paris, in order to induce their civil servants to go to work in the colonies, created for those amenable to the idea a grand quality of life. A minor clerk from the post office in Manchester received upon arrival in Tanganyika a villa with a garden and swimming pool, cars, servants, holidays in Europe, etc. Members of the colonial bureaucracy lived truly magnificently. And now, between one day and the next, the inhabitants of the colony receive their independence. They take over the colonial state in an unaltered form. They even take great care not to alter anything, because such a state offers fantastic privileges, which its new administrators naturally do not wish to renounce. The colonial origins of the African state – a state wherein the civil servant received renumeration beyond all measure and reason – ensured that in independent Africa, the struggle for power instantly assumed an extremely fierce and ruthless character. All at once, in the blink of an eye, a new ruling class arises – a bureaucratic bourgeoisie that creates nothing, produces nothing, but merely governs the society and reaps the benefits. The twentieth-century principle of vertiginous speed applied in this instance as well – once, decades, even centuries, were needed for a new social class to emerge, and here all it took was several days. The French, who were observing the struggle for positions with some wry amusement, called the phenomenon *la politique du ventre* (politics of the belly), so closely was a political appointment connected with huge material gains.

But this is Africa, and the fortunate nouveau riche cannot forget the old clan tradition, one of whose supreme canons is share everything you have with your kinsmen, with another member of your clan, or, as they say here, with your cousin. (In Europe, the bond with a cousin is by now rather weak and distant, whereas in Africa a cousin on your mother's side is more important than a husband.) So – if you have two shirts, give him one; if you have a bowl of rice, give him half. Whoever breaks this rule condemns himself to ostracism, to expulsion from the clan, to the horrifying status of outcast. Individualism is highly prized in Europe, and perhaps nowhere more so than in America; in Africa, it is synonymous with unhappiness, with being accursed. African tradition is collectivist, for only in a harmonious group could one face the obstacles continually thrown up by nature. And one of the conditions of collective survival is the sharing of the smallest thing. One day a group of children surrounded me. I had a single piece of candy, which I placed in my open palm. The children stood motionless, staring. Finally, the oldest girl took the candy, bit it into pieces, and equitably distributed the bits.

If someone has become a government minister, replacing a white man, and has received his villa, garden, salary, and car, word of this quickly reaches this fortunate one's place of origin. It spreads like wildfire to neighbouring villages. Joy and hope well up in the hearts of his cousins. Soon they begin their pilgrimage to the capital. Once here, they easily locate their distinguished distant relative. They appear at the gate of his house, greet him, ritualistically sprinkle the ground with gin to thank the ancestors for such a felicitous turn of events, and then make themselves at home in the villa, in the yard, in the garden. Before long, we can observe how the quiet residence where an elderly Englishman lived with his taciturn wife is now noisily teeming with the new official's kinsmen. From the earliest morning, a fire is going in front of the house, women are mashing cassava in wooden mortars, a gaggle of children are romping among the flower beds and borders. In the evenings, the entire extended family sits down to dinner on the lawn – for although a new life has begun, an old custom from the days of unremitting poverty remains: one eats only once a day, in the evening.

Whoever has a more mobile occupation, and less respect for tradition, tries to cover his tracks. In Dodoma, I once ran into a street vendor hawking oranges who used to bring these fruits to my house in Dar es Salaam. I was happy to see him, and asked him what he was doing here, five hundred kilometres from the capital. He had had to flee from his cousins, he explained. He had shared his meagre profits with them for a long time, but finally had had enough, and ran. 'I will have a few cents for a while,' he said happily. 'Until they find me again!'

Social advancements of this type are still relatively infrequent in Dar es Salaam in the years immediately following independence. In the white neighbourhoods, whites still dominate. For Dar es Salaam, like other cities in this part of the continent, consists of three distinct quarters, separated from one another either by water or by a stretch of bare ground.

The best neighbourhood, close to the sea, belongs of course to the whites. It is called Oyster Bay: magnificent villas, gardens exploding with flowers, thick lawns, smooth, gravel-strewn avenues. Yes, you can live truly luxuriously here, especially since you don't have to do anything yourself: everything is taken care of by quiet, vigilant, discreetly moving servants. Here, a man ambles along as he probably would do in paradise: slowly, loosely, content that he is here, enchanted by the beauty of the world.

Beyond the bridge, on the other side of the lagoon, significantly farther from the sea, lies a paved-over, crowded, busy, mercantile neighbourhood. Its inhabitants are Indians, Pakistanis, natives of Goa, arrivals from Bangladesh and Sri Lanka, all of them collectively called Asians here. Although there are several men of great wealth among them, the majority are middle class, living without any excess. They are traders. They buy, sell, act as middlemen, speculate. They are always counting something, counting endlessly, shaking their heads, quarrelling. Dozens, hundreds of shops, wide open, their goods spilling out onto the pavements, onto the streets. Fabrics, furniture, lamps, pots and pans, mirrors, knickknacks, toys, rice, syrups, spices – everything. In front of a shop sits a Hindu, one foot resting on the seat of his chair, his fingers digging at his toes.

Every Saturday afternoon, the inhabitants of this airless, swarming neighbourhood go to the seashore. They dress in their finest clothes – the women in golden saris, the men in neat shirts. They travel by car. The whole family piles in, perched on one another's laps, shoulders, heads – ten, fifteen people. They stop the car on the steep slope above the ocean. At this time of day, the incoming tide pounds the beach with powerful, deafening waves. They open the windows. They breathe in the salty smell. They air themselves. On the other side of the immense body of water before them lies their country, which some don't even know anymore: India. They spend fifteen minutes here, maybe a half hour. Then the convoy drives off and the shore is empty again.

The farther from the sea, the greater the heat, the aridity, and the dust. It is there, on the dry sand, on the bare, barren earth, that stand the clay huts of the African quarter. Its individual neighbourhoods bear the names of the old slave villages of the sultan of Zanzibar: Kariakoo, Hala, Magomeni, Kinondoni. The names may vary, but the quality of their clay houses is uniformly low, and their standard of living wretched, with no prospect of improvement.

For the people of those neighbourhoods, independence means being free to walk at will the main streets of this city of more than a hundred thousand, and even to venture into the white areas. It was never really forbidden, because the African could always turn up there, but he had to have a clear, concrete goal: he either had to be going to work, or going home from work. The policeman's eye easily distinguished between the gait of someone hurrying to some task and purposeless, suspicious loafing. Everyone, depending on the colour of his skin, had his assigned role and prescribed place.

Those who wrote about apartheid emphasized that this was a system invented and enforced in South Africa, a state governed by white racists. But apartheid is a much more universal, common phenomenon. Its critics maintained that it is a system instituted by rabid Boers so that they could rule indivisibly and keep the blacks in the ghettos, which were called bantustans. The ideologists of apartheid defended themselves: we believe that all people are entitled to better their circumstances and to develop, but, depending on the colour of their skin and their ethnicity, to develop separately. This was a piece of fraudulence, for whoever knew the reality understood that behind this support for equal development lay a deeply inequitable and unjust state of affairs: the whites possessed the best plots of land and the cities' richest neighbourhoods, and they controlled industry, while the blacks were consigned to crowded, wretched scraps of semi-arid land.

The concept of apartheid was so perverse that with time its principal victims began to discover certain advantages in it, a chance for a kind of self-reliance, the comfort of being in one's own backyard. The African could say: 'It is not only I, the black man, who cannot enter your area, but you, too, the white man, if you want to stay in one piece and not place yourself in danger, you had better not come into my neighbourhood!'

It was in such a city that I arrived as the correspondent of the Polish Press Agency, and in which I was to spend several years. Going about its streets, I quickly realized I was in the net of apartheid. First of all, the issue of skin colour suddenly loomed large. In Poland, in Europe, I never thought about it. Here, in Africa, it was becoming the most important determinant of my identity, and for simple people, the sole one. The white man. White, therefore a colonialist, a pillager, an occupier. I subjugated Africa, conquered Tanganyika, put to the sword the entire tribe of the man just now standing before me, the tribe of his ancestors.

I made him an orphan. Moreover, a humiliated and powerless orphan. Eternally hungry and sick. Yes, when he looks at me, this is exactly what he must be thinking: the white man, the one who took everything from me, who beat my grandfather on his back, who raped my mother. Here he is before me, let me take a good look at him!

I could not adequately resolve the question of guilt. In their eyes, I was guilty. Slavery, colonialism, five hundred years of injustice – after all, it's the white men's doing. The white men's. Therefore mine. Mine? I was not able to conjure within myself that cleansing, liberating emotion – guilt; to show contrition; to apologize. On the contrary! From the start, I tried to counter-attack: 'You were colonized? We, Poles, were also! For one hundred and thirty years we were the colony of three foreign powers. White ones, too.' They laughed, tapped their foreheads, walked away. I angered them, because they thought I wanted to deceive them. I knew that despite my inner certainty about my own innocence, to them I was guilty. These barefoot, hungry, and illiterate boys had a moral advantage over me, the sole advantange an accursed history bestows upon its victims. With rare exceptions, they, the black men, had never conquered anybody, hadn't occupied, hadn't enslaved. They could regard me from a position of superiority. They were of a black race, but a pure one. I stood among them weak, with nothing more to say.

I didn't feel comfortable anywhere. The colour of my skin, albeit privileged, also confined me to the cage of apartheid. A gilded cage – Oyster Bay – but a cage nonetheless. Oyster Bay is a beautiful neighbourhood. Beautiful, blooming with flowers – and boring. Granted, one could stroll here amid tall palm trees, admire the billowing bougainvillea and the elegant, delicate tuberose, the cliffs covered with thick seaweed. But what else? Besides this, what? The residents of the neighbourhood were colonial bureaucrats, who thought only of getting to the end of their contract, buying a crocodile skin or a rhinoceros horn as a souvenir, and leaving. Their wives discussed either the children's health or a past or upcoming party. And I had a daily story to file! About what? Where would I get the material? There was one small local newspaper, the *Tanganyika Standard*. I visited its editorial offices, but the staff consisted of these very same Englishmen from Oyster Bay. And they too were already packing.

I went to the Indian quarter. But what was I to do here? Where was I to go? Who was there for me to talk to? The heat was dreadful, and it was impossible to walk for any length of time: there is no air to breathe, your legs grow weak, your shirt drips with sweat. After an hour of wandering around, you are fed up with everything. You have but one desire left: to sit down somewhere in the shade. Better yet, beneath a fan. And then a thought strikes you: do the inhabitants of the North appreciate what a treasure they possess in that grey, drab, perpetually cloudy sky, with its one great, miraculous advantage – that there is no sun in it?

My main goal, of course, was the African suburbs. I had their names written down. I had the address for the office of the ruling party, TANU (Tanganyika

African National Union). But I couldn't find it. Identical streets, sand up to your ankles, children who won't let you pass, crowding around you, amused, aggressively curious – a white man in these inaccessible back alleys is a sensation and a spectacle. With each step I lose my confidence. I feel the attentive gaze of men sitting idly in front of houses, following me with their eyes. The women don't look, turning their heads away: they are Muslims, dressed in black, loosely draped gowns called bui-bui, which completely conceal their bodies as well as part of their faces. The irony of the situation is that even if I were to strike up a conversation with one of the Africans and wished to talk further to him, we would have nowhere to go. The good restaurant is for Europeans, the bad one for Africans. They never frequent each other's establishments; it isn't the custom. Each one would feel ill at ease if he found himself in a place inconsistent with the dictates of apartheid.

Now that I had a powerful, four-wheel-drive vehicle, I could set off. And there was reason to: in early October, a neighbour of Tanganyika's, Uganda, was gaining its independence. The wave of liberation was sweeping the entire continent: in one year alone, 1960, seventeen African countries ceased being colonies. And this process was continuing, though at a diminished pace.

From Dar es Salaam to Uganda's capital, Kampala, where the ceremony was to take place, is three days' solid driving, going from dawn to dusk at maximum speed. Half the route is asphalt, the other half consists of reddish laterite roads, called African graters because they have a crenellated surface over which you can only drive fast, so as to skim over the tops of the crenellations.

A Greek went along with me, Leo – a part-time broker, part-time correspondent for various Athenian newspapers. We took four spare tyres, two barrels of gasoline, a barrel of water, food. We set out at dawn, heading north, to the right of us the Indian Ocean, invisible from the road, to the left first the massif of Nguro, and then, for the rest of the way, the plain of the Masai. Both sides of the road are dense with greenery. Tall grasses, thick, fleecy shrubs, spreading umbrella trees. It's this way all the way to Kilimanjaro and the two little towns nearby, Moshi and Arusha. In Arusha we turned west, towards Lake Victoria. Two hundred kilometres on, the problems started. We drove onto the enormous plain of the Serengeti, the largest concentration of wild animals on earth. Everywhere you look, huge herds of zebras, antelopes, buffalo, giraffes. And all of them are grazing, frisking, frolicking, galloping. Right by the side of the road, motionless lions; a bit farther, a group of elephants; and farther still, on the horizon, a leopard running in huge bounds. It's all improbable, incredible. As if one were witnessing the birth of the world, that precise moment when the earth and sky already exist, as do water, plants, and wild animals, but not yet Adam and Eve. It is this world barely born, the world without mankind and hence also without sin, that one can imagine one is seeing here.

The Cobra's Heart

This mood of elation quickly dissipated in the face of the realities and riddles of the journey. The first, most important question was, which way should we go? For when we emerged onto the great plain, what was heretofore a single broad trail suddenly forked into several identical-looking dirt paths, all leading in entirely different directions. And no guidepost, sign, or arrow in sight. The plain smooth as a tabletop, overgrown with tall grasses, no mountains or rivers, no natural orientation points of any kind, only this unending, increasingly unreadable, tangled net of trails.

There weren't even any intersections, but every few kilometres, sometimes every few hundred metres, more and more radiating tentacles, coils, and knots, from which secondary offshoots of the same kind branched out chaotically this way and that.

I asked Leo what he thought we should do, but he just looked about uncertainly and answered my question with an identical one. We drove on randomly, choosing roads that seemed to head west (and therefore towards Lake Victoria), but whichever the road, suddenly, after several kilometres and for no apparent reason, it would begin to turn in some unknown direction. Utterly confused, I would stop the car, wondering, now where? It was an especially urgent question, since we had neither a detailed map nor even a compass.

Soon, a new difficulty developed, for noontime arrived, and with it the hours of the greatest heat, when the world sinks into insensibility and silence. Animals seek shelter in the shade of trees. But the herds of buffalo have nowhere to hide. They are too large, too numerous. Each might be a thousand strong. Such a herd, in the hour of the greatest heat, simply grows motionless, dead still. It so happens that one has frozen this way precisely on the road along which we want to drive. We approach. Before us stand a thousand dark, granite-like statues, firmly set on the ground, as if petrified.

A mighty force slumbers in the herd, mighty and – should it explode anywhere near us – deadly. It is the force of a mountain avalanche, only inflamed, frenzied, driven by foaming blood. The zoologist Bernhard Grzimek tells of flying a small plane over the Serengeti and observing for months on end the behaviour of buffalo. A lone buffalo didn't react at all to the whir of the descending plane: it calmly continued grazing. When Grzimek flew over a large herd, however, it was different. It sufficed for there to be among them a single overly sensitive one, a hysteric, a hothouse flower, who at the sound of the engine would start to thrash around waiting to flee. The entire herd would immediately panic and, in terror, begin to move.

And here is just such a herd. What should we do? Stop and stand? For how long? Turn around? It's too late for that; I am afraid to turn around, for they might rush us. They are fantastically swift, stubborn, and persistent animals. I make a sign of the cross and slowly, slowly, in first gear, the clutch only half engaged, drive into the herd. It is enormous, stretching almost to the horizon. I observe the bulls, who are at the head. Those who are standing in the path of the car begin drowsily, sluggishly to step aside so that the car can pass. They do not move even a centimetre farther than is absolutely necessary, and still the Land Rover is constantly scraping against their sides. I am drenched in sweat as we drive through this minefield. Out of the corner of my eye I look at Leo. His eyes are shut. One metre after another, metre by metre. The herd is silent. Immobile. Hundreds of pairs of dark, bulging eyes in massive heads, filmy, dull, expressionless. The passage lasts a long time, a crossing seemingly without end, but at last we emerge on the other shore – the herd is now behind us, its deep, dark stain against the green surface of the Serengeti growing smaller and smaller.

The more time passed, the farther we drove, circling and straying, the more anxious I became. We had not encountered any people since morning. We had also not come upon either a larger road or any kind of signpost. The heat was terrifying, and it intensified with every minute, as if the road we were on, and all others as well, led directly towards the sun, and as we drove we were inexorably approaching the moment we would be consumed by fire, like offerings laid at its altar. The burning air started to quiver and undulate.

Everything was becoming fluid, each view blurred and washed out as in a film left running out-of-focus. The horizon receded and smudged, as if subject to the oceanic law of ebb and flow. The dusty grey parasols of the acacias swayed rhythmically and moved about – as if some confused madmen were tossing them here and there, at a loss for anything better to do.

But the worst by far was that the tangled net of roads that had held us in its treacherous and suffocating grip for several hours now itself twitched and began to move. I could see that the web, the entire intricate geometry, which admittedly I had not been able to decipher but which nonetheless was a kind of constant, a fixed element upon the surface of the savannah, was now thrashing about and drifting. Where was it drifting to? Where was it pulling us, entwined in its coils? We were all being swept somewhere, Leo, the car and I, the roads, the savannah, the buffalo, and the sun, towards some unknown, shining, white-hot space.

Suddenly, the engine stopped and the car came to an abrupt halt. Leo, seeing that something was wrong with me, had turned off the ignition. 'Give it to me,' he said. 'I'll drive.' We continued this way until the heat diminished, and it was then that we spotted two African huts in the far distance. We drove up. They were empty, with no doors or windows. There were some wooden bunks inside. The houses clearly did not belong to anyone, and were simply intended for travellers who happened by.

I don't know how I found myself on one of the bunks. I was half dead. My head was pounding from the sun. To overcome drowsiness, I lit a cigarette. It didn't taste good. I wanted to put it out, and when I looked at my hand, which was reaching instinctively for the ground, I saw that I was about to extinguish the cigarette on the head of a snake lying under the bed.

I froze. Froze to such a degree that instead of quickly pulling back my hand, I left it suspended, cigarette burning, over the snake's head. Slowly, the reality of my position dawned on me: I was the prisoner of a deadly reptile. I knew one thing for certain: I could not move a muscle, because then the snake would attack. It was an Egyptian cobra, yellowish grey, neatly coiled on the floor. Its venom brings death quickly, and in our situation – with no medicines, and the nearest hospital probably a day's driving away – death would be inevitable. It was possible that at that very moment the cobra was in a state of light catalepsy (a condition of numbness and lethargy apparently typical of these reptiles), because it did not stir. My God, what should I do? I thought feverishly, by now completely wide awake.

'Leo,' I whispered loudly. 'Leo, a snake!'

Leo had been in the car, getting our luggage out. We stared at each other silently, not knowing how to proceed. Yet time was running out: were the cobra to awaken, it would probably attack instantly. Because we had no weapons of any kind, not even a machete, we decided that Leo would get a metal canister from the car and with it we would try to crush the cobra. It was a risky plan, but it was all we could come up with. We had to do something. Our inaction was giving the snake an advantage.

The canisters, from old British army supplies, were large, with sharp, protruding edges. Leo, who was a powerful man, grabbed one and started to creep towards the hut. The cobra was still just lying there, motionless. Leo, grasping the canister by its handles, lifted it up and waited. He was calculating, positioning himself, aiming. I lay still as stone on the bunk, tense, ready. And then suddenly, in a split second, Leo, holding the canister before him, threw his entire weight upon the snake. At which moment I too fell with my whole body on top of him. In these seconds, our lives hung in the balance – we knew this. Actually, we only thought of it later, for the instant the canister, Leo, and I came down on top of the snake, the interior of the hut exploded.

I never suspected there could be so much power within a single creature. Such terrifying, monstrous, cosmic power. I had assumed that the canister's edge would easily cut through the snake – nothing of the kind! I now saw we had beneath us not a snake, but a throbbing, vibrating steel spring, impossible to either break or crush. The cobra was thrashing and pounding the ground with such demented fury that the hut's interior grew dark from the dust. Under the powerful blows of its tail, the clay floor was crumbling and scattering, blinding us with clouds of debris. At one point it suddenly occurred to me with horror that we wouldn't manage, that the reptile would slip out from under us and, in pain, wounded, enraged, would start to bite us. I pressed down even harder on my friend. He was groaning, his chest crushed against the canister, unable to breathe.

Finally, but this took a long time, an eternity, the cobra's blows started to lose their impetus, vigour, frequency. 'Look,' Leo said. 'Blood.' Indeed, into a crevice along the floor, which now resembled a shattered clay dish, a narrow trickle of blood was slowly seeping. The cobra was weakening, and the vibrations of the canister, which we felt the whole time and by means of which the snake signalled us about her pain and her hatred, vibrations that terrified and panicked us, were also diminishing. But now, when it was all over, when Leo and I rose and the dust began to settle and thin out and I gazed down again at the narrow ribbon of blood being quickly absorbed, instead of satisfaction and joy I felt an emptiness inside, and something else as well: I felt sad that that heart, which inhabited the very pit of hell we had all shared through a bizarre coincidence only a moment ago, that that heart had stopped beating.

The next day we stumbled upon a wide, rust-coloured track that, in a wide arc, circumscribed Lake Victoria. Driving several hundred kilometres through a green, luxuriant, fertile Africa, we reached the Ugandan border. It wasn't really a border. A simple shed stood by the side of the road, with the sign 'Uganda' burned out on a wooden board above the door. The shed was empty and shuttered. The kinds of borders for which blood is spilled were still to come into being.

We drove on. Night had already fallen. Everything that in Europe is called dusk and evening here lasts only a few minutes, if it exists at all. It is daytime, and then night, as if someone has turned off the sun's generator with one flip of the switch. All at once, all is black. In one instant we are inside the night's darkest core. If this change surprises you as you are walking through the bush, you must stop immediately: you can see nothing, as if somebody has unexpectedly pulled a sack over your head. You become disoriented, you don't know where you are. In such darkness people converse without seeing one another. They might call out to one another, not realizing they are standing side by side. The darkness separates people, and thereby intensifies all the more their desire to be together, in a group, in a community.

The first hours of the night are the most social time in Africa. No one wants to be alone then. Being alone? That's misfortune, perdition! Children don't go to sleep early here. We enter the land of dreams together – as a family, a clan, a village.

We drove through an already sleeping Uganda, invisible behind the curtain of night. Somewhere nearby must have been Lake Victoria, somewhere the kingdoms of Ankole and Toro, the pastures of Mubende, Murchison Falls. All this surrounded by a night black as soot. A night full of silence. The car's headlights pierced the darkness, and in their glow whirled a frenzied swarm of little flies, beetles, and mosquitoes, which appeared as if out of nowhere, for a fraction of a second played out before our eyes their role of a lifetime – the insect's demonic dance – before perishing, splattered mercilessly upon the windshield of the speeding car.

Every now and then an oasis of light appeared in the undifferentiated blackness – a roadside shack lit up colourfully as though at a fair, glittering from afar: an Indian shop, a *duka*. Above the mounds of biscuits, tea bags, cigarettes, and matches, over the cans of sardines and the sticks of butter, we could make out, illuminated by a fluorescent lamp, the head of the proprietor, who sat motionless, waiting with patience and hope for late clients. The glow of these shops, which seemed to appear and disappear as if at our command, lit for us, like solitary lampposts on an empty street, the whole road to Kampala.

Kampala was readying for celebration. In several days, on October 9, Uganda was to receive its independence. The complicated deals and manoeuvres continued up to the very last minute. Everything about the internal politics of Africa's states is intricate and entangled. This stems directly from the fact that European colonialists, dividing Africa among themselves under Bismarck's leadership during the Berlin conference, crammed the approximately ten thousand kingdoms, federations, and stateless but independent tribal associations that existed on this continent in the middle of the nineteenth century within the borders of barely forty colonies. Meantime, many of these kingdoms and tribal groups shared a long history of conflict and wars. And here, without being asked their opinion on the matter, they suddenly found themselves within one and the same colony, subject to the same (and foreign) authority, the same laws.

Now, with decolonization, the old interethnic relationships, which European rule only froze or simply ignored, suddenly sprang back to life and were becoming relevant again. The chance for liberty appeared, yes, but liberty with a proviso: that yesterday's opponents and enemies form one nation and become its joint managers, patriots, and defenders. The former European colonial capitals and the leaders of Africa's independence movements adopted the principle that if bloody internal conflicts erupted within a given colony, that territory would not become free.

The process of decolonization was to occur through what were stipulated as constitutional methods, at a round table, without great political dramas, ensuring the preservation of that which was most important: the uninterrupted flow of goods and riches between Africa and Europe.

The circumstances under which the leap to the kingdom of liberty was to be accomplished presented many Africans with a difficult choice. Colliding within them were two sets of considerations, two loyalties, in painful, almost insoluble conflict. On the one hand lay the deeply encoded remembrance of the history of one's clan and people, of the allies one could turn to in times of need and of the enemies one had to despise, and on the other hand was the awareness that one was supposed to be entering the community of independent, modern societies, a precondition of which was the renunciation of all ethnic egoism and blindness.

It is this very problem that existed in Uganda. As defined by its current borders, it was a young country, barely several decades old. But its territory encompassed parts of four ancient kingdoms: Ankole, Buganda, Bunyoro, and Toro. The history of their mutual animosities and conflicts was as colourful and rich as anything between the Celts and the Saxons, or the Montagues and the Capulets.

Preeminent among them was the kingdom of Buganda, whose capital, Mengo, made up one of Kampala's neighbourhoods. Mengo is also the name of the hill upon which the royal palace stands. For Kampala, a city of extraordinary beauty, full of flowers, palm trees, mango trees, and poinsettia, is laid out across seven gentle green hills, several of which descend directly to the lake.

Once, royal palaces kept springing up on these hills, one by one: when a king died, his residence was abandoned and a new one was built on the next hilltop. The object was to not disturb that ongoing rule of the deceased, which continued, albeit from the other world. Thus the entire dynasty held power at once, with the actual living king as its guardian, its temporary representative.

In 1960, two years prior to liberation, people who did not consider themselves subject to the king of Buganda formed the UPC party (Uganda People's Congress), which won the first elections. At its head stood a young civil servant, Milton Obote; I met him while he was still in Dar es Salaam.

The journalists who were expected in Kampala were to live in the barracks of an old hospital, situated slightly outside of town (the new one, a gift from

Queen Elizabeth, was awaiting its dedication). We were the first to arrive; the barracks, white and clean, were still empty. In the main building, I was handed the room key. Leo was driving north to see Murchison Falls. I envied him, but had to stay behind to gather some material for my story. I found my building, which stood at some remove, on a slope amid luxuriant cinnamon and tamarind trees. The entrance to the room was at the end of a long corridor. I walked in, set down my bag and suitcase, closed the door. And at that moment I noticed that the bed, table, and chest of drawers were rising, and high up, beneath the ceiling, starting to whirl faster and faster.

I lost consciousness.

Inside the Mountain of Ice

When I opened my eyes, I saw a large white screen, and against its brightness the face of a black girl. Her eyes observed me for a moment, then vanished together with the rest of her face. A moment later the head of an Indian appeared on the screen. He must have leaned over me, for suddenly I saw him in close-up, as if magnified many times over.

'Thank God, you're alive,' I heard. 'But you're sick. You have malaria. Cerebral malaria.'

I came to instantly. I wanted to sit up, but felt that I didn't have the strength to, that I was paralysed. Cerebral malaria is the terror of tropical Africa. Once, it was inevitably fatal. Even now it is dangerous, and frequently still deadly. Driving here, we passed near Arusha a cemetery of its victims, a vestige of the epidemic that had passed that way several years ago.

I tried to look around. The white screen above me was the ceiling of the room in which I was lying. I was in the just-opened Mulago Hospital, one of its first patients. The girl was a nurse called Dora, and the Indian was a doctor, Patel. They told me that an ambulance called by Leo had brought me here the day before. Leo had gone to the north, seen Murchison Falls, and three days later returned to Kampala. He walked into my room and saw me lying there unconscious. He ran to the reception desk for help, but it was Uganda's independence day, the entire town was dancing, singing, swimming in beer and palm wine, and poor Leo didn't know what to do. Finally he drove to the hospital himself and arranged for an ambulance. And that is how I found myself here, in a private room, in which everything still smelled of freshness, peace, and order.

The first signal of an imminent malaria attack is a feeling of anxiety, which comes on suddenly and for no clear reason. Something has happened to you, something bad. If you believe in spirits, you know what it is: someone has pronounced a curse, and an evil spirit has entered you, disabling you and rooting you to the ground. Hence the dullness, the weakness, the heaviness that comes over you. Everything is irritating. First and foremost, the light; you hate the light. And others are irritating – their loud voices, their revolting smell, their rough touch.

But you don't have a lot of time for these repugnances and loathings. For the attack arrives quickly, sometimes quite abruptly, with few preliminaries. It is a sudden, violent onset of cold. A polar, arctic cold. Someone has taken you, naked, toasted in the hellish heat of the Sahel and the Sahara, and thrown you straight into the icy highlands of Greenland or Spitsbergen, amid the snows, winds, and blizzards. What a shock! You feel the cold in a split second, a terrifying, piercing, ghastly cold. You begin to tremble, to quake, to thrash about. You immediately recognize, however, that this is not a trembling you are familiar with from earlier experiences – say, when you caught cold one winter in a frost; these tremors and convulsions tossing you around are of a kind that at any moment now will tear you to shreds. Trying to save yourself, you begin to beg for help.

What can bring relief? The only thing that really helps is if someone covers you. But not simply throws a blanket or quilt over you. This thing you are being covered with must crush you with its weight, squeeze you, flatten you. You dream of being pulverized. You desperately long for a steamroller to pass over you.

I once had a powerful malaria attack in a poor village, where there weren't any heavy coverings. The villagers placed the lid from some kind of wooden chest on top of me and then patiently sat on it, waiting for the worst tremors to pass. The most wretched are those who have a malaria attack and there is nothing to wrap them in. You can see them by the roadsides, in the bush, or in the clay huts, lying semicomatose on the ground, drenched in sweat, confused, their bodies rent by rhythmic waves of malarial convulsions. But even snuggled under a dozen blankets, jackets, and coats, your teeth chatter and you moan with pain, because you sense that this cold does not come from without – it's forty degrees Celsius out there! – but that it's within, inside you, that these Greenlands and Spitsbergens are in you, that all those floes, sheets, and mountains of ice are advancing through your veins, muscles, and bones. Perhaps this thought would fill you with fear – were you able to summon the strength to feel anything at all. But the thought occurs just as the peak of the attack, after several hours, is gradually subsiding, and you start a helpless descent into a state of extreme exhaustion and weakness.

The malaria attack is not merely painful, but like every pain also a mystical experience. We enter a realm about which a moment ago we knew nothing, though it now turns out that it had existed alongside us all the while, finally capturing and incorporating us: we discover within ourselves icy crevasses, chasms, and abysses, whose presence fills us with suffering and fear. But this moment of discovery, too, passes, the spirits desert us, depart, and disappear, and that which remains, under the mountain of the most bizarre coverings, is truly pitiful.

A man right after a strong attack of malaria is a human rag. He lies in a puddle of sweat, he is still feverish, and he can move neither hand nor foot. Everything hurts; he is dizzy and nauseous. He is exhausted, weak, limp. Carried by someone else, he gives the impression of having no bones or muscles. And many days must pass before he can get up on his feet again.

Each year in Africa malaria afflicts tens of millions of people, and in those areas where it is most prevalent – in wet, low-lying, marshy regions – it kills one child out of three. There are many types of malaria; some, the gentle ones, you should be able to recover from as you would from the flu. But here, even those can lay waste whoever succumbs to them. First, because in this murderous climate one endures with difficulty even the slightest indisposition; second, because Africans are often malnourished, attenuated, hungry. Time and again you encounter here drowsy, apathetic, benumbed people. They sit or lie for hours on end on the streets, by the roadsides, doing nothing. You speak to them and they do not hear you; you look at them and have the impression that they do not see you. It is unclear if they are ignoring you, if these are just idle lazybones and do-nothings, or if they are being ravaged by a malaria that is slowly and inexorably killing them. You do not know how to behave toward them, or what to think.

I lay for two weeks in the Mulago Hospital. The attacks recurred, but each one less intense and exhausting than the preceding. I got countless injections. Dr Patel came every day, examined me, told me that when I was better he would introduce me to his family. He has a wealthy family, owners of large stores in Kampala and in the provinces. They were able to educate him in England, and he received his medical degree in London. How did his ancestors come to find themselves in Uganda? At the end of the nineteenth century, his grandfather and thousands of other young Indians were brought by the English to eastern Africa to build the railway line from Mombasa to Kampala. It was a new phase of colonial expansion: the conquest and subjugation of the continent's interior. If you look closely at old maps of Africa, you will notice a peculiarity: inscribed along the coastlines are dozens, hundreds of names of ports, cities, and settlements, whereas the rest, a vast 99 percent of Africa's surface, is a blank, essentially virgin area, only sparsely marked here and there.

The Europeans clung to the coasts, to their ports, eating houses, and ships, reluctantly and only sporadically making incursions into the interior. They were hampered by the lack of roads, fearful of hostile tribes and tropical diseases – malaria, sleeping sickness, yellow fever, leprosy. And although they inhabited the coasts for more than four centuries, they did so in a spirit of impermanence, with a narrow-minded goal of quick profits and easy spoils. Their ports were really only leeches on the body of Africa, points of export for slaves, gold, and ivory. Their goal: to carry away everything, and at the lowest possible price. Consequently, many of these European beachheads resembled the poorest sections of old Liverpool or Lisbon. In the course of four hundred years in Luanda, the Portuguese did not dig a single well for potable water, or illuminate the streets with lanterns.

The construction of the railway line to Kampala was the symbol of a new, more paternalistic approach to Africa on the part of the colonial powers, especially London and Paris. With the division of Africa among the European states already securely accomplished, they could turn their attentions to investing in those parts of their colonies whose rich and fertile soils held the promise of huge profits from coffee, tea, cotton, and pineapple plantations, or, in other places, from diamond, gold, or copper mines. But there were no means of transport. The old way – porters carrying everything on their heads – no longer sufficed. Roads, railway lines, and bridges had to be built. Yes, but who would do this? They could not bring in white workers:

the white man was master here, he could not do physical labour. Initially, the local African worker was also out of the question: he simply did not exist. It was impossible to induce the local population to work for wages, because they didn't yet understand the concept of money (for centuries, trade here was based on barter, and one paid for slaves, for example, with firearms, lumps of salt, calico fabrics).

With time, the British introduced a system of forced labour: the tribal chief had to supply a given number of people to work for free. They were placed in camps. Large concentrations of these gulags indicated places where colonialism had settled for good. Before this occurred, however, other quick alternatives had to be found. One of them was to import to eastern Africa cheap labour from another British colony: India. In this way Dr Patel's grandfather found himself first in Kenya, and then in Uganda, where he later settled permanently.

During one of his visits, the doctor told me how in the course of the railroad's construction, when the tracks began to draw away from the shores of the Indian Ocean and enter the vast territories covered with dense bush, terror began spreading among the Hindu workers: lions had started to attack them.

A lion in his prime does not like to hunt humans. He has his own predatory customs, his favourite tastes and gustatory preferences. He loves the meat of antelope and zebra. He also likes giraffe, although they are difficult to hunt, being so tall and large. And he doesn't turn his nose up at beef, which is why at night shepherds gather their herds within enclosures built in the bush out of thorny branches. But even such a fence is not always an effective barrier, for the lion is a superb jumper and can soar over the goma, as they call it, or just as adroitly crawl under it.

Lions hunt at night, usually in a pride, organizing approaches and ambushes. Immediately before a hunt, a division of roles takes place. There are those who are in charge of driving the prey, directing it towards the jaws of the executioners. The lionesses are the most active, and it is they who attack most frequently. The males are the first to feast: they slurp the freshest blood, swallow the most tender morsels, lick up the fatty marrow.

The daytime hours are spent digesting and sleeping. The lions lie drowsily in the shade of the acacias. If one doesn't irritate them, they will not attack. Even if one approaches them, they will get up and walk farther away. This is a risky manoeuvre, however, for a predator like this can execute a leap in a split second. Once, on the drive across the Serengeti, we got a flat tyre. Instinctively I jumped out of the car to change it, and suddenly realized that around us in the tall grass, next to the bloody shreds of an antelope, lay several lionesses. They watched us but didn't move. Leo and I sat shut in the car, waiting, wondering what they would do. After a quarter of an hour they rose and, tawny, shapely, beautiful, calmly ambled off into the bush.

Lions going forth to hunt announce this with a mighty roar that carries over the entire savannah. The sound frightens, panics the other animals. Only elephants are oblivious to these battle horns: elephants are not afraid of anyone. The others scatter wherever they can, or else stand, paralysed with terror, waiting until the predator emerges from the darkness and delivers the mortal blow.

The lion is an efficient and formidable hunter for about twenty years. After that he begins to show his age. His muscles weaken, his speed diminishes, his leaps grow shorter. It is difficult for him to chase down a skittish antelope, a swift and vigilant zebra. He walks around hungry, a burden to the pride. It is a dangerous moment for him – the pride does not tolerate the weak and the ill, and he can fall prey to it himself. More and more frequently, he fears that the younger ones will bite him to death. He gradually detaches himself from the pride, lags behind, and finally is alone. He is tormented by hunger, but can no longer chase game. He has only one recourse: to hunt humans. Such a lion is commonly referred to here as a man-eater, and he terrorizes the local population. He lurks near streams where women go to do the wash, near paths along which children walk to school (being hungry, he now hunts by day as well). People are afraid to walk out of their huts, but he attacks them there, too. He is fearless, merciless, and still relatively strong.

It was lions like these, Dr Patel continued, that started to attack the Indians building the railway line to Kampala. The men slept in cotton tents, which the predators easily slashed to pieces as they pulled out a steady supply of victims. No one protected these people, and they didn't have their own guns. In any event, to battle a lion in the African darkness is a losing proposition. The doctor's grandfather and his companions heard at night the screams of men being torn apart, for the lions feasted fearlessly, in close proximity to the tents, and then, sated, vanished into the gloom.

The doctor always found time for me and conversed willingly, for which I was grateful since even several days after an attack I would still be unable to read, the print blurring, the letters swimming about, as if lifted up and rocked on invisible waves.

'Have you seen a lot of elephants already?' he asked me once.

'Oh, hundreds,' I answered.

'And do you know,' he said, 'that long ago, when the Portuguese first arrived here and started buying up ivory, they were struck by the fact that Africans didn't have a great deal of it. Why, they wondered? After all, the tusks are very rugged and long-lasting, and if it is difficult for them to hunt down a live elephant for its ivory – they usually did this by chasing the animal into a hole they had dug earlier – then why don't they collect the tusks from elephants that have already died, and whose corpses are doubtless lying somewhere? They suggested this idea to their African middlemen, but heard something astonishing by way of reply: there are no dead elephants, there are no elephant cemeteries. The Portuguese were intrigued. How do elephants die? Where are their remains? At issue were the tusks, the ivory, and the large sums of money they commanded.

'The manner in which elephants die was a secret Africans long guarded from the white man. The elephant is sacred, and so is his death. Everything sacred is surrounded by an impenetrable mystery. What caused the elephant to be so admired was that he had no enemies in the animal world. No other beast could conquer him. He could die (in the past) only a natural death. It occurred usually at dusk, when the elephants came to the water. They would stand at the edge of a lake or river, reach out far with their trunks, and drink. But the day would come when a tired old elephant could no longer raise his trunk, and to drink clear water he would have to walk farther and farther out into the lake. His legs would sink into the muck, deeper and deeper. The lake pulled him into its cavernous interior. He fought for a time, thrashed about, attempted to extricate himself from the bog and get back to the shore, but his own weight was so great, and the pull of the lake's bottom so paralysing, that finally the animal would lose its balance, fall, and vanish under the water forever.

'There,' Dr Patel finished, 'on the bottoms of our lakes, are the age-old elephant cemeteries.'

The Anatomy of
a Coup d'État

From a notebook I kept in Lagos in 1966:

On Saturday, January 15, the army staged a *coup d'état* in Nigeria. At one o'clock in the morning, an alarm sounded in all the military units across the country. The various divisions set about carrying out their designated tasks. The difficulty of the *coup* lay in its needing to be implemented in five cities at once: in Lagos, which is the capital of the federation, as well as in the capitals of Nigeria's four regions – in Ibadan (Western Nigeria), Kaduna (Northern Nigeria), Benin (Central-Western Nigeria), and Enugu (Eastern Nigeria). In a country with a surface area three times that of Poland, inhabited by fifty-six million people, the *coup* was executed by an army numbering barely eight thousand soldiers.

Saturday, 2 a.m.

Lagos: Military patrols (soldiers in helmets, battle dress, and carrying automatic weapons) seize control of the airport, the radio station, the telephone exchange, and the post office. By orders of the military, the electrical plant cuts power to the African neighbourhoods. The city sleeps, the streets are empty. Saturday night is very dark, hot, and airless. Several jeeps stop near King George V Street. It is a small street at one tip of the island of Lagos (for which the whole city is named). On one side is the stadium. On the other – two villas. One is the residence of the prime minister of the federation, Sir Abubakar Tafawa Balewa. In the other lives the minister of finance, Chief Festus Okotie-Eboh. The soldiers surround both villas. A group of officers enters the prime minister's residence, wakes him, and leaves with him. A second group arrests the minister of finance. The cars drive off. Several hours later, an official government communiqué will state that the prime minister and his appointee 'were taken to an unknown destination'. Balewa's subsequent fate is unknown. Some say he is imprisoned in the military barracks; many believe he has been killed. People maintain that Okotie-Eboh was also killed. He was not shot, they say, but rather 'bludgeoned to death'. This version may be less a reflection of reality than an expression of public opinion about the man. He was a deeply repugnant individual, brutal, greedy, large, even grotesquely fat. Through corruption, he managed to amass an indescribably large fortune. He behaved with the utmost contempt towards the people he ostensibly served. Balewa was his opposite – likeable, modest, calm. A tall, thin, almost ascetic Muslim.

The army seizes the harbour and surrounds Parliament. Patrols circulate through the streets of the sleeping city.

It is 3 a.m.

Kaduna: On the outskirts of the capital of Northern Nigeria, surrounded by high walls, stands the one-storey residence of the region's prime minister, Ahmadu

Bello. In Nigeria, the titular head of state is Dr Nnamdi Azikiwe. The head of the government, Tafawa Balewa. But the actual ruler of the country is Ahmadu Bello. All Saturday long Bello receives guests. The last visit, at 7 p.m., is paid him by a group of Fulani. Six hours later, in the bushes across from the residence, a group of officers sets up two mortars. The group's commander is Major Chukuma Nzeogwu. At three o'clock in the morning, a shot is fired from a mortar. The shell explodes on the roof of the residence. A fire erupts. It is the signal to attack. The officers first storm the palace's guardhouse. Two of them die in the struggle with the prime minister's security force, the rest make it into the flaming building. In the hallway they encounter Ahmadu Bello, who has run out of his bedroom. He is felled by a bullet, which hits him in the temple.

The city sleeps, the streets are empty.

It is 3 a.m.

Ibadan: The palace of the prime minister of Western Nigeria, Chief Samuel Akintola, stands on one of the gentle hills over which sprawls this single-storeyed city-village, 'the largest village in the world', with 1.5 million inhabitants. For three months now, bloody battles have been waged in the region, a police curfew is in effect in the city, and Akintola's palace is heavily guarded. The troops begin their assault, a gun battle ensues, and then outright hand-to-hand combat. A group of officers finally forces its way into the palace. Akintola dies on the verandah, hit by thirteen bullets.

*

It is 3 a.m.

Benin: The army commandeers the radio station, the post office, and other important targets. It closes all exits from the city. Several officers disarm the policemen guarding the residence of the region's prime minister, Chief Dennis Osadebay. Not a shot is fired. From time to time, a green jeep carrying soldiers passes down the street.

It is 3 a.m.

Enugu: The residence of the prime minister of Eastern Nigeria, Dr Michael Okpara, is silently and discreetly surrounded. Inside, in addition to the prime minister, sleeps his guest, the president of Cyprus, Archbishop Makarios. The commander of the insurgents guarantees both dignitaries their freedom of movement. In Enugu, the revolution is polite. Other army units seize the radio station, the post office, and close off all roads exiting the city, which continues to sleep.

The *coup* was successfully carried out in five Nigerian cities simultaneously. In the space of several hours, the small army became the *de facto* ruler of this enormous country – Africa's superpower. In the course of a single night, death, arrest, or flight into the bush ended hundreds of political careers.

Saturday – morning, afternoon, and evening.

Lagos awakes, knowing nothing about anything. A normal city day begins – the shops open, people are on their way to work. There is no visible army presence downtown. But at the post office we are told that all lines of communication with the outside world have been severed. You cannot send a telegram. The first bits of gossip start to circulate around the city. That Balewa was arrested. That the army staged a *coup d'état*. I drive to the barracks in Ikoyi (a Lagos neighbourhood). Jeep patrols are coming out of the gates, armed with automatic weapons, with machine guns. A crowd has gathered across from the gate, motionless, silent. Women who eke out a living cooking and selling simple dishes on the street are already spreading out in a smokey encampment.

At the other end of town, Parliament convenes. There are many soldiers in front of the building. They search us at the entrance. Out of the 312 members of Parliament, only 33 have arrived. Only one minister appears – R. Okafor. He proposes that the deliberations be postponed. The representatives who are present demand explanations: What has happened? What is happening? At this, a military patrol enters the chamber – eight soldiers, who disperse the assembled.

The radio broadcasts only music. There are no announcements. I go to see the AFP correspondent, David Laurell. We are both close to tears. These are frustrating moments for journalists: we have news of world import, and we cannot transmit it. We set off together for the airport. It is guarded by a division of the navy and appears deserted – no passengers, no aeroplanes. On the way back we are stopped at a military checkpoint: they will not let us back into town. A long discussion ensues. The soldiers are polite, courteous, calm; an officer arrives and eventually waves us through. We return through dark neighbourhoods: there is still no electrical power. The pavement vendors are burning candles or oil lamps near their stalls, as a result of which the streets look from a distance like cemetery alleyways on the Day of the Dead. Even at night it is humid, and so airless that it is difficult to breathe.

Sunday – new rulers.

Helicopters buzz over the city, but otherwise the day is peaceful. Such a revolt (and they are more and more frequent) is usually orchestrated by a small group of officers living in barracks inaccessible to civilians. They act with the utmost secrecy. The country learns of everything after the fact, and then most often has to rely on gossip and conjecture.

This time, however, the situation is quickly clarified. Just before midnight, the new head of state – Major General Johnson Aguiyi-Ironsi, the 41-year-old army commander – goes on the radio. He says that the military 'consented to take power', that the constitution and the government are being suspended. Power will now lie with the Supreme Military Council. Law and order will be restored in the country.

Monday – the reasons for the *coup*.

Rejoicing in the streets. My Nigerian friends, meeting me, slap me on the back, laugh; they are in excellent spirits. I walk through the square – the crowds are dancing, a boy beats out a rhythm on an aluminium barrel. A month ago, I witnessed a similar *coup d'état* in Dahomey – there, too, the street was cheering the army. The latest wave of military revolts is very popular in Africa; reaction is enthusiastic.

The first expressions of support and of allegiance to the new government arrive in Lagos: 'The day of January 15,' says the resolution of one of the local parties, the UPGA (United Progressive Grand Alliance), 'will pass into the history of our great republic as the day when we first achieved true liberty, although Nigeria has been independent for five years now. The mad rush of our politicians toward self-enrichment disgraced Nigeria's name abroad . . . A ruling caste had arisen in our country, which based its power on the sowing of hatred, on pitting brother against brother, on liquidating everyone who held a view different from theirs . . . We salute the new regime as if it had been sent down by God to liberate the nation from black imperialists, from tyranny and intolerance, from the deceptions and destructive ambitions of those who claimed to represent Nigeria . . . Our Motherland cannot be a stomping ground for political wolves, who plunder the country.'

'The widespread anarchy and the disillusion of the masses,' states the resolution of the youth organization, Zikist Movement, 'made this revolution necessary. In the years since independence, fundamental human rights were brutally violated by the government. People were denied the right to live in freedom and with mutual respect. They were not allowed to have their own opinions. Organized political gangsterism and the politics of falsehood turned all elections into a farce. Instead of serving the nation, politicians were busy stealing. Unemployment and exploitation were on the rise, and in their sadism toward the population, the small clique of feudal fascists in power knew no bounds.'

Thus many African nations are already living through a second phase of their short postwar history. The first phase was a rapid decolonization, the gaining of independence. It was characterized by a universal optimism, enthusiasm, euphoria. People were convinced that freedom meant a better roof over their heads, a larger bowl of rice, a first pair of shoes. A miracle would take place – the multiplying of loaves, fishes, and wine. Nothing of the sort occurred. On the contrary. There was a sudden increase in the population, for which there was not enough food, schools, or jobs. Optimism quickly turned to disenchantment and pessimism. The people's bitterness, fury, hatred was now directed against their own elites, who were rapidly and greedily stuffing their pockets. In a country without a well-developed private sector, where plantations belonged to foreigners and the banks to foreign capital, the political career was the only road to riches.

In short – the poverty and disillusion of those on the bottom rungs, coupled with the cupidity and gluttony of those on the top, create a poisoned, unstable atmosphere, which the army senses; presenting itself as the champion of the injured and the humiliated, it emerges from the barracks and reaches for power.

*

Tuesday – the tom-toms call to war.

A report from Eastern Nigeria that appeared in today's edition of the Lagos newspaper, the *Daily Telegraph*:

Enugu.   When news of the arrest of the prime minister of Eastern Nigeria, Dr Michael Okpara, reached his native region of Bende, in all the local villages – in Ohuku, Ibeke, Igbere, Akyi, Ohafia, Abiriba, Abam, and Nkporo – the war drums began to beat, convening the tribal warriors. They were told that their compatriot, Dr Okpara, had been kidnapped. At first, the warriors believed this was the work of the agents of the ruling coalition, and decided to go to war. Anyone who owned a wagon put it at their disposal. In the course of a few hours, Enugu, the capital of Eastern Nigeria, was overrun by fighters armed to the teeth with swords, spears, bows, and shields. The warriors chanted war songs. Tom-toms pounded throughout the town. As this was going on, it was explained to the tribal commanders that it was the army that had seized power, and that Dr Okpara was alive, although under house arrest. When the warriors heard this, they expressed joy and began returning to their villages.

Thursday, January 20 – the journey to Ibadan.

I went to Western Nigeria to find out what people were saying about the revolution. At the Lagos tollgates, soldiers and policemen inspect cars and baggage. It is 150 kilometres from Lagos to Ibadan, along a green-lined road running between gentle hills. In recent months, during the civil war, many people died here. You still never know whom you will meet around the next curve. In the ditches lie burned-out cars, most often large limousines with governmental licence plates. I stopped near one of them – there were still charred bones inside. All the towns along the road bear the signs of battle: the skeletons of houses incinerated, or levelled; furniture broken, trucks turned upside down, smouldering ruins. Every place is deserted, the people have run away, scattered who knows where.

I reach Akintola's villa. It is on the outskirts of Ibadan, in a residential, wooded ministerial neighbour-hood, now completely abandoned. The palaces of the ministers, imposing, luxurious, and kitschy, stand ruined and empty. Even the servants are gone. Some of the ministers have died, others fled to Dahomey. There are several policemen in front of Akintola's place. One of them grabs a gun before giving me a tour. The villa is large, new. A puddle of blood has congealed on the marble floor at the entrance. A bloodied djellabah is still lying next to it. There is a pile of scattered, torn letters, and two plastic machine guns, smashed to pieces, perhaps belonging to Akintola's grandsons. The walls are pockmarked by bullet holes, the courtyard full of shattered glass, the window screens ripped out by soldiers during the assault on the villa.

Akintola was fifty years old, a heavyset man with a wide, baroquely tattooed face. In the past several months he had not left his residence, which was under heavy police guard – he was afraid. Five years ago he had been a middle-class lawyer. After a year of premiership, he already had millions. He simply poured money from the government accounts into his private ones. Wherever you go in Nigeria, you come across his houses – in Lagos, in Ibadan, in Abeokuta. He had twelve limousines, largely unused, but he liked to look at them from his balcony. His ministers also grew rich quickly. We are here in a realm of absolutely fantastical fortunes, all made in politics, or, more precisely, through political gangsterism – by breaking up parties, falsifying election results, killing opponents, firing into hungry crowds. One must see this wealth against the background of desperate poverty, in the context of the country over which Akintola ruled – burned, desolate, awash in blood.

I returned to Lagos in the afternoon.

Saturday, January 22 – Balewa's funeral.

The announcement by the Federal Military Government about the death of the former prime minister of Nigeria, Sir Abubakar Tafawa Balewa:

On Friday morning peasants from the region of Otta, near Lagos, said that they had found in the bush a corpse resembling Tafawa Balewa. It was in a sitting position, its shoulders leaning against a tree. The body was covered by an ample white djellabah, and a round cap was lying at its feet. That same day the body was transported by special plane to Balewa's native town of Bauchi (in Central Nigeria). Besides the pilot and the radio operator, there were only soldiers on board. The body of Tafawa Balewa was buried in the Muslim cemetery in the presence of a large number of people.

The daily *New Nigerian* states that the inhabitants of Northern Nigeria do not believe in the death of their leader, Ahmadu Bello. They are convinced that he escaped under Allah's coat to Mecca.

Today a friend, a Nigerian student named Nizi Onyebuchi, told me: 'Our new leader, General Ironsi, is a supernatural man. Someone was shooting at him and the bullet changed course, not so much as grazing the General.'

Amin

I once considered writing a book about Amin, because he is such a glaring example of the relation between crime and low culture. I was in Uganda many times, saw Amin more than once; I have a small library of books about him, and stacks of my own notes. He is the most well known dictator in the history of contemporary Africa and one of the most famous in the twentieth century the world over.

Amin belongs to a small ethnic group called the Kakwa, whose territory encroaches on three countries: Sudan, Uganda, and Zaire. The Kakwa do not know to which country they belong, although they view this question with indifference, preoccupied as they are with something else: how to survive despite the poverty and hunger that prevail in this remote region without roads, cities, electricity, and cultivable land. Anyone with some initiative, wits, and luck runs as far away from here as possible. But not every direction is a propitious one. Whoever goes west will only worsen his circumstances, because he will stumble upon the thickest jungles of Zaire. Those setting off northward also err, because they will arrive at the sandy, rock-strewn threshold of the Sahara. Only the southerly direction holds promise: there the Kakwa will find the fertile lands of central Uganda, the lush and splendid garden of Africa.

It is there, after giving birth to her son, that Amin's mother makes her way, the infant on her back. She comes to the second-largest city (or, rather, town) in Uganda after Kampala – Jinja. Like thousands of others at that time, and millions upon millions today, she arrives in the hope of surviving, in the hope that life here will be better. She has no skills, no contacts, and no money. But one can make a living in a variety of ways: through petty trade, brewing and selling beer, or operating a portable pavement eatery. Amin's mother has a pot and cooks millet in it. She sells portions on banana leaves. Her daily earnings? A serving of millet for herself and her son.

This woman, who made her way with her child from a poor village in the north to a town in the wealthier south, became part of the population that today constitutes Africa's biggest problem. It is composed of the tens of millions who have abandoned the countryside and migrated to the monstrously swollen cities without securing adequate housing or employment. In Uganda they are called *bayaye*. You will notice them at once, because it is they who form the street crowds, so different from ones in Europe. In Europe, the man on the street is usually heading toward a definite goal. The crowd has a direction and a rhythm, which is frequently characterized by haste. In an African city, only some of the people behave this way. The others are not going anywhere: they have nowhere to go, and no reason to go there. They drift this way and that, sit in the shade, stare, nap. They have nothing to do. No one is expecting them. Most often, they are hungry. The slightest street spectacle – a quarrel, a fight, the apprehension of a thief – will instantly draw large numbers of them. For they are everywhere around here, idle, awaiting who knows what, living who knows how – the gapers of the world.

The principal characteristic of their status is rootlessness. They will not return to the countryside, and there is no place for them in the city. They endure. Somehow, they exist. Somehow: that is how best to describe their situation, its fragility, its uncertainty. Somehow one lives, somehow one sleeps, somehow, from time to time, one eats. This unreality and impermanence of existence cause the *bayaye* to feel himself in continuous danger, and so he is unceasingly tormented by fear. His fear is amplified by his condition as a stranger, an unwanted immigrant from another culture, religion, language. A foreign, extraneous competitor for the contents of the cooking pot, which is empty anyway, and for work, of which there isn't any.

Amin is a typical *bayaye*.

He grows up in the streets of Jinja. The town housed a battalion of the British colonial army, the King's African Rifles. The model for this army was devised towards the end of the nineteenth century by General Lugard, one of the architects of the British Empire. It called for divisions composed of mercenaries recruited from tribes hostile towards the population on whose territory they were to be garrisoned: an occupying force, holding the locals on a tight rein. Lugard's ideal soldiers were young, well-built men from the Nilotic (Sudanese) populations, which distinguished themselves by their enthusiasm for warfare, their stamina, and their cruelty. They were called Nubians, a designation that in Uganda evoked a combination of distaste and fear. The officers and non-commissioned officers of this army, however, were for many years exclusively Englishmen. One day, one of them noticed a young African with a Herculean physique hanging around the barracks. It was Amin. He was quickly enlisted. For people like him – without a job, without possibilities – military service was like winning the lottery. He had barely four years of elementary schooling, but because he was deemed obedient and eager to anticipate the wishes of his commanders, he began advancing rapidly through the ranks. He also gained renown as a boxer, becoming the Ugandan heavyweight champion. During colonial times, the army was dispatched on countless expeditions of oppression: against the Mau Mau insurgents, against the warriors of the Turkana tribe, or against the independent people of the Karimojong. Amin distinguished himself in these campaigns: he organized ambushes and attacks, and was merciless towards his adversaries.

It is the fifties, and the era of independence is fast approaching. Africanization has arrived, even in the military. But the British and French officers want to remain in control for as long as possible. To prove that they are irreplaceable, they promote the third-rate from among their African subordinates, those not too quick, but obedient, transforming them in a single day from corporals and sergeants into colonels and generals.

Bokassa in the Central African Republic, for example, Soglo in Dahomey, Amin in Uganda.

When in the fall of 1962 Uganda becomes an independent state, Amin is already, because of promotions by the British, a general, and deputy commander of the army. He takes a look around him. Although he has high rank and position, he comes from the Kakwa, a small community and one, moreover, that is not regarded as native Ugandan. Meantime, the preponderance of the army comes from the Langi tribe, to which Prime Minister Milton Obote belongs, and from the related Acholi. The Langi and the Acholi treat the Kakwa superciliously, seeing them as benighted and backward. We are navigating here in the paranoid, obsessive realm of ethnic prejudice, hatred, and antipathy – albeit an intra-African one: racism and chauvinism emerge not only along the most obvious divides, e.g., white versus black, but are equally stark, stubborn, and implacable, perhaps even more so, among peoples of the same skin colour. Indeed, most whites who have died in the world have died at the hands not of blacks, but of other whites, and likewise the majority of black lives taken in the past century were taken by other blacks, not by whites. And so it follows, for example, that on account of ethnic bigotry, no one in Uganda will care whether Mr XY is wise, kind, and friendly, or the reverse, evil and loathsome; they will care only whether he is of the tribe of Bari, Toro, Busoga, or Nandi. This is the sole criterion by which he will be classified and evaluated.

For its first eight years of independence, Uganda is

ruled by Milton Obote, an extraordinarily conceited man, boastful and sure of himself. When it is exposed in the press that Amin has misappropriated the cash, gold, and ivory given him for safekeeping by anti-Mobutu guerrillas from Zaire, Obote summons Amin, orders him to pen an explanation, and, confident that he himself is in no danger, flies off to Singapore for a conference of prime ministers of the British Commonwealth. Amin, realizing that the prime minster will arrest him as soon as he returns, decides on a preemptive strike: he stages an army *coup* and seizes power. Theoretically at least, Obote in fact had little to worry about: Amin did not represent an obvious threat, and his influence in the army was ultimately limited. But beginning on the night of January 25, 1971, when they took over the barracks in Kampala, Amin and his supporters employed a brutally efficient surprise tactic: they fired without warning. And at a precisely defined target: soldiers from the Langi and Achole tribes. The surprise had a paralysing effect: no one had time to mount a resistance. On the very first day, hundreds died in the barracks. And the carnage continued. Henceforth, Amin always used this method: he would shoot first. And not just at his enemies; that was self-evident, obvious. He went further: he liquidated without hesitation those he judged might one day develop into enemies. Over time, terror in Amin's state also came to depend on universal torture. Before they died, people were routinely tormented.

All this took place in a provincial country, in a small

town. The torture chambers were located in downtown buildings. The windows were open – we are in the tropics. Whoever was walking along the street could hear cries, moans, shots. Whoever fell into the hands of the executioners vanished. A category soon emerged, then grew and grew, of those who in Latin America are called *desaparecidos:* those who have perished, disappeared. He left his house and never returned. '*Nani?*' the policemen routinely replied, if a family member demanded an explanation. '*Nani?*' (In Swahili the word means 'who'; the individual reduced to a question mark.)

Uganda started to metamorphose into a tragic, bloody stage upon which a single actor strutted – Amin. A month after the *coup* Amin named himself president, then marshal, then field marshal, and finally field marshal for life. He pinned upon himself ever more orders, medals, decorations. But he also liked to walk about in ordinary battle fatigues, so that soldiers would say of him, 'You see, he's one of us.' He chose his cars in accordance with his outfits. Wearing a suit to a reception, he drove a dark Mercedes. Out for a spin in a sweat suit? A red Maserati. Battle fatigues? A military Range Rover. The last resembled a vehicle from a science-fiction movie. A forest of antennas protruded from it, all kinds of wires, cables, spotlights. Inside were grenades, pistols, knives. He went about this way because he constantly feared attempts on his life. He survived several. Everyone else died in them – his *aides-de-camp*, his bodyguards. Amin alone would brush off the dust, straighten his uniform. To cover his tracks, he also rode in unmarked cars. People walking down a street would suddenly realize that the man sitting behind the wheel of that truck was Amin.

He trusted no one, therefore even those in his innermost circle did not know where he would be sleeping tonight, where he would be living tomorrow. He had several residences in the city, several more on the shores of Lake Victoria, still others in the countryside. Determining his whereabouts was both difficult and dangerous. He communicated with every subordinate directly, decided whom he would speak with, whom he wished to see. And for many, such a meeting would prove the last. If Amin became suspicious of someone, he would invite him over. He would be pleasant, friendly, treat his guest to a Coca-Cola. Executioners awaited the visitor as he left. Later, no one could determine what had happened to the man.

Amin usually telephoned his subordinates, but he also used the radio. Whenever he announced changes in the government or in the ranks of the military – and he was constantly instituting changes – he would do so over the airwaves.

Uganda had one radio station, one small newspaper (*Uganda Argus*), one camera, which filmed Amin, and one photojournalist, who would appear for ceremonial occasions. Everything was directed exclusively at the figure of the marshal. Moving from place to place, Amin in a sense moved the state with him; outside of him, nothing happened, nothing existed. Parliament did not exist, there were no political parties, trade unions, or other organizations. And, of course, no opposition – those suspected of dissent died painful deaths.

Amin's support was the army, which he created according to the colonial model, the only one he knew. Most of the men came from small communities inhabiting Africa's remote peripheries, lands on the border of Uganda and Sudan. They spoke Sudanese languages, in contrast to the country's native population, which is Bantu-speaking. Simple and uneducated, they were unable to communicate. But that was the intention – they felt alien, isolated, and wholly dependent on Amin. Whenever a truckful of them arrived, panic would erupt, the streets would empty, the villages grow deserted. Savage, enraged, most often drunk, the soldiers would pillage what they could, beat whomever they could. Randomly, indiscriminately. In the market, they would seize the sellers' goods. (If there were any, that is, for the Amin years were a time of empty shelves. As I was leaving for Kampala once, someone advised me to take along a lightbulb – there would be power in the hotel, but no bulbs.) The soldiers stole the peasants' crops, cattle, chickens. One constantly heard them shouting, '*Chakula! Chakula!*' (in Swahili, food, eat). Only copious amounts of food – a side of beef, an entire bunch of bananas, a large bowl of beans – would appease them and then for only a brief moment.

Amin was in the habit of visiting garrisons scattered across the country. On such occasions, a rally would be organized in the square. The marshal would speak. He liked to speak for hours on end. As a surprise, he would bring with him some notable person, a civilian or a military man, whom he suspected of treason, of conspiracy, of a coup attempt. The accused, bound with ropes, earlier already roughed up and scared out of his wits, was hauled to the dais. The crowd, excited by the sight, would fall into a trance and start to howl. 'What shall I do with him?' Amin would try to make himself heard above the din. And the throng would shout: 'Kill him! Kill him!'

The troops were in constant battle readiness. Amin, who had earlier given himself the title Conqueror of the British Empire, decided that he would liberate those among his brethren still languishing in the chains of colonial slavery. He began a series of onerous and costly military manoeuvres. His troops practised liberating the Republic of South Africa. Battalions attacked 'Pretoria' and 'Johannesburg', the artillery strafed enemy positions in 'Port Elizabeth' and 'Durban'. Amin observed the hostilities through a pair of binoculars from the terrace of a villa dubbed the Command Post. Irritated by the slowness of the battalion from Jinja to capture 'Cape Town', he would jump into a car and, agitated, in a lather, drive from one command point to the other, berating the officers, inciting the rank and file to battle. The shells plunged into Lake Victoria, sending up plumes of water and terrifying the fishermen.

He was a man of inexhaustible energy, perpetually excited, always in motion. When, as president, he occasionally convened a session of government, he was able to participate in it only briefly. He would soon grow bored, leap up from his chair, and leave. His thoughts came fast and furiously; he spoke chaotically, did not complete his sentences. He read English with difficulty, and was not proficient in Swahili. He had a solid command of his Kakwa dialect, although few Ugandans spoke it. Yet it is precisely these short-comings that made him popular among the *bayaye*: he was like them, blood of their blood, bone of their bone.

Amin had no friends, and did not allow anyone to know him for long or intimately, fearful that such a relationship might enable others to organize a con-spiracy or a *coup*. In particular, he frequently changed the heads of the two secret police units, the Public Safety Unit and State Research Bureau, which he had created for the express purpose of terrorizing the country. In the latter served *bayaye* from related Sudan-ese peoples – the Kakwa, the Lugabra, the Madi, and their kinsmen, the Nubians. The SRB sowed fear in Uganda. Its strength stemmed from the fact that each of its members had direct access to Amin.

One day I was wandering around the market in Kam-pala. It was somewhat empty, many stalls were broken, abandoned. Amin had stripped and ruined the country. There was no traffic in the streets, and the shops, which Amin had earlier confiscated from their Indian owners, gaped with musty emptiness or were simply boarded up with wooden planks, plywood, or sheets of tin. Suddenly, a band of children came up the street that led up from the lake, calling, '*Samaki! Samaki!*' (fish in Swahili). People gathered, joyful at the prospect that there would be something to eat. The fishermen threw their catch onto a table, and when the onlookers saw it, they grew still and silent. The fish was fat, enormous. These waters never used to yield such monstrously proportioned, overfed specimens. Everyone knew that for a long time now Amin's henchmen had been dumping the bodies of their victims into the lake, and that crocodiles and meat-eating fish must have been feasting on them. The crowd remained quiet. Then, a military vehicle happened by. The soldiers saw the gathering, as well as the fish on the table, and stopped. They spoke for a moment among themselves, then backed up to the table, jumped down, and opened the tailgate. Those of us who were standing nearby could see the corpse of a man lying on the truck bed. We saw the soldiers heave the fish onto the truck, throw the dead, barefoot man onto the table for us, and quickly drive away. And we heard their coarse, lunatic laughter.

Amin's rule lasted eight years. According to various sources, the field marshal for life murdered between 150,000 and 300,000 people. Finally, he provoked his own downfall. One of his obsessions was his hatred for the president of neighbouring Tanzania, Julius Nyerere. Towards the end of 1978, he attacked Tanzania. The Tanzanian army responded. Nyerere's troops entered Uganda. Amin escaped to Libya, before he was allowed to settle in Saudi Arabia, as a reward for services in propagating Islam. Amin's army dispersed, some of his troops returning to their homes, others taking up banditry. The losses suffered by the Tanzanian army? One tank.

The Black Crystals of the Night

The orange ball of the sinking sun is just visible at the far end of the road along which we are driving. It will disappear at any moment behind the horizon and cease blinding us, and then night will descend, rapidly, and we will be left alone with the dark. Out of the corner of my eye I notice that Sebuya, the driver of the Toyota, is growing anxious. In Africa, drivers avoid travelling at night – darkness unnerves them. They are so afraid of it that they may flatly refuse to drive after sunset. I have observed them at times when they were nevertheless compelled to do so. Instead of keeping their eyes focussed straight ahead, they begin to peer apprehensively to the sides. Their features grow tense and sharp. Beads of sweat appear on their brows. They fidget in their seats, and slide down behind the steering wheel as if someone were shooting at the car. Despite the fact that the roads are rough, full of potholes, washouts, and ruts, instead of slowing down, they accelerate, tearing carelessly along, anything just to reach a place where there are people, where one can hear the hum of human voices and where the lights are shining.

'*Kuna nini?*' I ask (in Swahili: did something bad happen?). They never answer, just careen along amid clouds of dust and the clang of metal.

'*Hatari?*' I ask after a while (some kind of danger?). They remain silent, paying no attention.

They are afraid of something, grappling with a demon that I do not see and do not understand. For me, this night has well-defined and straightforward characteristics: it is dark, almost black, hot, windless, and, if we stop and Sebuya turns off the engine, full of silence. But according to Sebuya, I know nothing of darkness. In particular, I do not know that day and night are two distinct realities, two separate worlds. In daytime, man can cope somehow with his environment, can exist and endure, even live peacefully; the night, however, renders him defenceless, easy prey to his enemies, and conceals forces with nefarious designs upon his life. That is why fear, which during the day slumbers in a man's heart, secretive and subdued, is transformed at night into an overpowering fright, a haunting, tormenting nightmare. How important it is at that time to be in a group! The presence of others brings relief, soothes the nerves, lessens the tension.

'*Hapa?*' (here?) Sebuya asked me, when we caught sight of the mud shacks of a village by the roadside. We were in western Uganda, not far from the Nile, driving towards the Congo. It was getting dark and Sebuya was already very jittery. I could see that I would be unable to persuade him to keep going, so agreed to spending the night here.

The villagers took us in without enthusiasm, even reluctantly, which is strange and surprising in these parts. But Sebuya pulled out a wad of shillings, and the sight of money, so extraordinary and tempting for these people, decided things in our favour. Before long, a cleanly swept clay hut lined with fresh grasses had been prepared for us. Sebuya fell quickly into a deep sleep, but I was soon awakened by an army of bustling and aggressive insects. Spiders, cockroaches, crickets, ants, a multitude of tiny, soundless, and busy creatures, which while often invisible, could be felt slithering, clinging, tickling, pinching – sleep was impossible. For a long time I turned from side to side, until finally, exhausted and defeated, I stepped out in front of the hut and sat down, leaning my back against the wall. The moon was shining brightly and the night was clear, silvery. All around was profound silence. Cars rarely appear in these parts, and the wildlife has long been killed off and eaten.

Suddenly, I heard murmurs, steps, then the rapid patter of bare feet. Then silence once more. I looked around, but at first saw nothing. After a moment, the murmurs and steps again. Then silence again. I began to study the features of the landscape – a clump of thin shrubs, several umbrella-shaped acacias in the distance, some rocks protruding from the ground. At last, I spied a group of eight men, carrying, on a simple stretcher made of branches, another man covered with a piece of cloth. They moved in a peculiar fashion. They did not walk in a straight line, but advanced furtively, creeping in one direction, then in another, manoeuvring. They crouched down behind a shrub, looked about cautiously, and then scurried to the next hiding place.

They circled, swerved, stopped, and started, as if they were children playing some elaborate game of espionage. I observed their bent, half-naked silhouettes, their nervous gestures, the queer, stealthful behaviour, until finally they disappeared for good behind a ridge, and the only thing around me again was the silent, clear, inviolate night.

At dawn we drove on. I asked Sebuya if he knew the name of the people in whose village we had spent the night. 'They are called Amba,' he said. Then, after a moment, added: '*Kabila mbaya*' (this means, roughly, 'bad people'). He did not want to tell me any more – here, one avoids evil even as a subject of conversation, preferring not to step into that territory, careful not to call the wolf out of the forest. As we drove, I reflected upon the event I had inadvertently witnessed. The nocturnal drama, those puzzling zigzags and twists of the bearers, their haste and anxiety, concealed a mystery to which I had no key. Something was going on here. But what?

People like the Amba and their kinsmen believe profoundly that the world is ruled by supernatural forces. These forces are particular – spirits that have names, spells that can be defined. It is they that inform the course of events and imbue them with meaning, decide our fate, determine everything. For this reason nothing happens by chance; chance simply does not exist. Let us consider this example: Sebuya is driving his car, has an accident, and dies. Why exactly did Sebuya have an accident? That very same day, all over the world, millions of cars reached their destinations safely – but Sebuya had an accident and died. White people will search for various causes. For instance, his brakes malfunctioned. But this kind of thinking leads nowhere, explains nothing. Because why was it precisely Sebuya's brakes that malfunctioned? That very same day, all over the world, millions of cars were on the road and their brakes were working just fine – but Sebuya's were not. Why? White people, whose way of thinking is the height of naivety, will say that Sebuya's brakes malfunctioned because he failed to have them inspected and repaired in good time. But why was it precisely Sebuya who failed to do this? Why, that very same day, a million . . . etc., etc.

We have now established that the white man's way of reasoning is quite unhelpful. But it gets worse! The white man, having determined that the cause of Sebuya's accident and death was bad brakes, prepares a report and closes the case. Closes it!? But it is precisely now that the case should begin! Sebuya died because someone cast a spell on him. This is simple and self-evident. What we do not know, however, is the identity of the perpetrator, and that is what we must now ascertain.

Speaking in the most general terms, a wizard did it. A wizard is a bad man, always acting with evil intent. There are two types of wizards (although our Western languages do not differentiate adequately between them). The first is more dangerous, for he is the devil in human form. The English call him witch. The witch is a dangerous person. Neither his appearance nor his behaviour betray his satanic nature. He does not wear special clothing, he does not have magical instruments. He does not boil potions, does not prepare poisons, does not fall into a trance, and does not perform incantations. He acts by means of the psychic power with which he was born. Malefaction is a congenital trait of his personality. The fact that he does evil and brings misfortune owes nothing to his predilections; it brings him no special pleasure. He simply is that way.

If you are near him, he need only look at you. Sometimes, you will catch someone watching you carefully, piercingly, and at length. It might be a witch, just then casting a spell on you. Still, distance is no obstacle for him. He can cast a spell from one side of Africa to the other, or even farther.

The second type of wizard is gentler, weaker, less demonic. Whereas the witch was born as evil incarnate, the sorcerer (for that is what this weaker sort is called in English) is a career wizard, for whom the casting of spells is a learned profession, a craft, and a source of livelihood.

To condemn you to illness or bring some other misfortune down on you, or even to kill you, the witch has no need of props or aids. All he need do is direct his infernal, devastating will to wound and annihilate you. Before long, illness will fell you, and death will not be far behind. The sorcerer does not have such destructive powers within himself. To destroy you, he must resort to various magical procedures, mysterious rites, ritual gestures. For example, if you are walking at night through thick bush and lose an eye, it is not because you accidentally impaled yourself on a protruding yet invisible branch. Nothing, after all, happens by accident! It is simply that an enemy of yours wanted to exact vengeance and went to see a sorcerer. The sorcerer fashioned a little clay figure – your likeness – and, with the tip of a juniper branch dipped in hen's blood, gouged out its eye. In this way he issued a verdict on your eye – cast a spell on it. If one night you are wending your way through dense bush and a branch pokes out your eye, it will be proof positive that an enemy of yours wanted to avenge himself, went to see a sorcerer, etc. Now it is up to you to uncover who this enemy is, go visit a sorcerer, and in turn order your own revenge.

If Sebuya dies in a car crash, then the most important thing for his family now is to ascertain not whether his brakes were bad, for that is of no consequence, but whether the spells that caused this death were cast by a wizard-devil (witch) or an ordinary wizard-craftsman (sorcerer). It is a critical question, entailing a long and intricate investigation, into which will be pressed various fortune-tellers, elders, medicine men, and so forth. The outcome of this detective work is of utmost significance! If Sebuya died as a result of spells cast by a wizard-devil, then tragedy has befallen the entire family and clan, because a curse like that affects the whole community, and Sebuya's death is merely a foretoken, the tip of the iceberg: there is nothing to do but await more illnesses and deaths. But if Sebuya perished because a wizard-craftsman wanted it thus, then the situation is far less dire. The craftsman can strike and destroy only individuals, isolated targets: the family and the clan can sleep in peace!

Evil is the curse of the world, and that is why I must keep wizards, who are its agents, carriers, and propagators, as far away from myself and my clan as possible; their presence poisons the air, spreads disease, and makes life impossible, turning it into its opposite – death. The wizard, by definition, lives and practises among others, in another village, in another clan or tribe. Our contemporary suspicion of and antipathy for the Other, the Stranger, goes back to the fear our tribal ancestors felt towards the Outsider, seeing him as the carrier of evil, the source of misfortune. Pain, fire, disease, drought, and hunger did not come from nowhere. Someone must have brought them, inflicted them, disseminated them. But who? Not my people, not those closest to me – they are good. Life is possible only among good people, and I am alive, after all. The guilty are therefore the Others, the Strangers. That is why, seeking retribution for our injuries and setbacks, we quarrel with them, enter into conflicts, conduct wars. In a word, if unhappiness has befallen us, its source is not within us, but elsewhere, outside, beyond us and our community, far away, in Others.

I had long forgotten about Sebuya, about our expedition to the Congo, and about the night spent in the Amba village, when years later, in Maputo, a book fell into my hands about magic in eastern Africa, specifically a report by the anthropologist E. H. Winter on studies he conducted among the Amba.

The Amba, Winter states, are a highly unusual social group. Like other tribes on the continent, they take seriously the existence of evil and the danger of spells, and thus fear and hate wizards, but contrary to the widely held view that wizards dwell among others, that they act from without, from a distance, the Amba maintain that the wizards are among them, within their families, within their villages, that they form an integral part of their community. This belief has resulted in the gradual disintegration of Amba society, corroded as it has become by hatred, consumed by suspicion, confounded by free-floating fear. Anyone can be a wizard, brother fears brother, son fears father, a mother fears her own children. The Amba rejected the comfortable and comforting view that the enemy is the stranger, the foreigner, the man of a different faith or skin colour. No! Possessed by a peculiar kind of masochism, the Amba live in torment and distress; at this very moment, evil can be under my own roof, asleep in my bed, eating from the same dish as I. And there is an additional difficulty: it is impossible to determine what wizards look like. After all, no one has seen one. We know they exist because we see the results of their actions: they caused the drought, as a result of which there is nothing to eat, fires keep igniting, many people are sick, someone is always dying. Plainly, wizards never rest, endlessly occupied as they are with raining misfortunes, defeats, and tragedies down upon our heads.

The Amba are a homogeneous, cohesive community

who live in small villages scattered in sparsely wooded bush; often they suspect a neighbouring village, inhabited by their kinsmen, of harbouring the wizard who has caused them misfortune. They declare war on the village they judge to be evil. The besieged community defends itself, and sometimes undertakes a war of retaliation. The unceasing wars the Amba wage among themselves leave them thoroughly weakened and defenceless against aggressors from other tribes. Nonetheless, they are so preoccupied with the internecine threat that they are oblivious to this danger. Paralysed by the spectre of an enemy within the gates, they tumble unrestrained into the abyss.

The depressing fate that has come to weigh upon them at least unites them, makes possible a paradoxical solidarity. If I become convinced, say, that a wizard hiding in my village is plaguing me, I can move to another one, and even if that village is at war with my own, I will be hospitably received. This is because all Ambas appreciate how much a wizard can torment you. Consider the paths along which you walk: he can scatter on them pebbles, leaves, feathers, little twigs, dead flies, monkey hairs, or mango peelings. It is enough merely to step on any one of those things – you will at once sicken and die. And such small nothings can be found on every trail. So, practically speaking, you cannot move? That is correct, you cannot. You are afraid even to step out of your mud house, for right there on the threshhold might be a piece of the bark of a baobab, or a poisoned acacia thorn.

The wizard wants to hound us to death – that is his

objective. There is no medicine against him, there is no protection. The only option is flight. That is why the people I saw that night, carrying a sick man on a stretcher, were moving so furtively: they were escaping. A wizard had cast a spell on the sick man, and the illness was a sign that the wizard was preparing the man's death. That is why the victim's relatives, under the cover of darkness, were trying to hide him, conceal him from the wizard's view, save his life.

Although no one knows what the wizard looks like, we know a lot about him. He moves only at night. He participates in ceremonies during which sentences are meted out – we are sleeping, and over there, unbeknownst to us, our demise has been decided. He can transport himself to wherever he wishes with fantastic speed, quicker than lightning. He adores human flesh, dotes on human blood. He does not speak, so we cannot recognize his voice. We do not know his facial features, the shape of his head.

But it is possible that one day a man will be born with such strength of vision and such willpower that, staring intently into the blackness, he will see the night begin to thicken, stiffen, coalesce into black crystals, and then will see these crystals compose themselves ever more clearly into the silent and dark visage of a wizard.

THE STORY OF PENGUIN CLASSICS

Before 1946 ... 'Classics' are mainly the domain of academics and students, without readable editions for everyone else. This all changes when a little-known classicist, E. V. Rieu, presents Penguin founder Allen Lane with the translation of Homer's *Odyssey* that he has been working on and reading to his wife Nelly in his spare time.

1946 *The Odyssey* becomes the first Penguin Classic published, and promptly sells three million copies. Suddenly, classic books are no longer for the privileged few.

1950s Rieu, now series editor, turns to professional writers for the best modern, readable translations, including Dorothy L. Sayers's *Inferno* and Robert Graves's *The Twelve Caesars*, which revives the salacious original.

1960s The Classics are given the distinctive black jackets that have remained a constant throughout the series's various looks. Rieu retires in 1964, hailing the Penguin Classics list as 'the greatest educative force of the 20th century'.

1970s A new generation of translators arrives to swell the Penguin Classics ranks, and the list grows to encompass more philosophy, religion, science, history and politics.

1980s The Penguin American Library joins the Classics stable, with titles such as *The Last of the Mohicans* safeguarded. Penguin Classics now offers the most comprehensive library of world literature available.

1990s The launch of Penguin Audiobooks brings the classics to a listening audience for the first time, and in 1999 the launch of the Penguin Classics website takes them online to a larger global readership than ever before.

The 21st Century Penguin Classics are rejacketed for the first time in nearly twenty years. This world famous series now consists of more than 1300 titles, making the widest range of the best books ever written available to millions – and constantly redefining the meaning of what makes a 'classic'.

The Odyssey continues ...

The best books ever written

PENGUIN (Ⓟ) CLASSICS

SINCE 1946

Find out more at www.penguinclassics.com